MW01254445

Helping Ourselves by Helping Each Other

THE LIFE STORY OF WILLIAM LYALL

Helping Ourselves by Helping Each Other

THE LIFE STORY OF WILLIAM LYALL

William Lyall

Edited by Louis McComber

Inuit Leadership and Governance

Volume Two

Inuit Leadership and Governance
Volume Two

Helping Ourselves by Helping Each Other
The Life Story of William Lyall

ISBN: 978-1-897568-13-2

Published by the Nunavut Research Institute.

Helping Ourselves by Helping Each Other was produced through a partnership between the Nunavut Research Institute, Laval University's CIERA (Centre interuniversitaire d'études et de recherches autochtones), Arctic Co-operatives Limited, and the Nunavut Department of Education. The book series entitled *Inuit Leadership and Governance* is part of a CIERA research project, *Inuit Leadership and Governance in Nunavut and Nunavik: Life Stories, Analytical Perspectives, and Training,* funded by the Social Sciences and Humanities Research Council of Canada, within its Community-University Research Alliance program.

For order information:
CIERA
Telephone: (418) 656-7596
ciera@ciera.ulaval.ca

Without the simple notion that helping each other makes life easier and better, we wouldn't be up here today.

Bill Lyall

William Lyall
President of Arctic Co-operatives Limited

Table of Contents

Foreword

The co-operative movement, particularly in English-speaking Canada, has not always been willing to recognize its leaders. This may be due to the fact that so many people within co-operatives have such deep commitments to grassroots activism; if one celebrates leaders too much, the contributions of the many may appear to be diminished. Perhaps it is the general tendency among English Canadians to refrain from celebrating the accomplishments of those with whom they work and live. Perhaps it is partly because most co-operative leaders have been unassuming and modest, and people honour most easily those who practically demand that recognition. Co-operative leaders are rarely charismatic figures, of the kind so evident in the cults of leadership that populate many business pages today, or who are so frequently featured in the leadership studies of business schools.

For whatever reasons, neither the movement nor many of those who have studied it have explored the contributions of many outstanding co-operative leaders. Many of these remarkable contributions, therefore, are not as prominent in the collective co-operative memory as one might wish. Names like Keen, Good, Staples, Morrison, Arnason, Walsh, Hannam, Harman, Ransom, Laidlaw, Melvin, Bromberger, and Craig are known and honoured by only a few within the movement. Given what the aforementioned people and many others have contributed, this is a major oversight. The movement, moreover, is weaker for not acknowledging and seeking to understand how such leaders achieved what they did.

Perhaps more importantly, these omissions suggest a problem within Co-operative Studies, at least as they are carried out in English-speaking Canada: a weakness in thinking about the issues associated with effective co-operative leadership. It is not a simple sort of leadership to analyse and understand; nor is it easily reduced to a single, all-encompassing theory, the kind so beloved in western intellectual traditions. There are many kinds of co-operatives, and each type has its own unique leadership requirements. The dynamics that characterize the activities of different co-operatives vary considerably, placing diverse demands upon their leaders. The variety of people one finds in co-operatives creates further challenges—trying to help fishing communities confronting declining fish stocks or Inuit who not long ago lived on the land are profoundly different activities compared with mobilizing the support of suburban consumers, for example. The types of businesses in which co-operatives are involved can impose different kinds of demands—insurance co-ops, for example, require different leadership skills and knowledge as compared to worker co-operatives. The stages of a given co-operative's development call out for different kinds of leadership—the leaders of the formative period are usually quite different from the leaders needed in mature co-operatives. It also makes a difference where a co-operative or a group of co-operatives is located—those in small communities on the Regina Plains have different needs and perspectives from those located in downtown Toronto, in Cape Breton, or on Baffin Island. Effective leadership within many co-operatives is subtle and diverse, far more so than is commonly recognized—even within the movement itself.

This book, therefore, is a very welcome addition to Co-operative Studies, particularly for people in English-speaking Canada. The subject, William "Bill" Lyall, richly deserves to be studied, and his work better understood. Along with his mentor and friend, Andrew Goussaert, he has played a crucial role in the development of the Arctic co-operatives in what used to be called the Northwest Territories and the Yukon. Their work, along with that which has been carried out by others in the communities of northern Québec, forms one of the most exciting developments in the Canadian and Québec movements of recent years. There is much to be learned from understanding why and how it happened, and from reflecting on what Bill Lyall attempted and what he has accomplished.

As this book so vividly demonstrates, the nature of Lyall's leadership needs to be understood from two different perspectives. One is the cultural context within which he has lived and worked; the other is the institutional frameworks through which he has made his contributions. This dichotomy is not unique to co-operative leadership, of course, but it is of fundamental importance to co-operatives because of the complex ways in which they relate to their communities and in how they conduct their democratic processes. The truth is that, while it is rarely acknowledged, co-operatives are organisations significantly shaped by the cultures within which they operate. One readily grasps the differences when one visits co-ops in different parts of the world; these differences are even apparent when one visits co-operatives in the various regions of Canada. Nowhere is it more obvious than when one visits northern co-operatives, the milieu in which Bill Lyall has lived and worked almost all of his life. Co-operatives do not function everywhere in the same way, though there is always a tendency to emphasize the similarities, despite the significant differences. Ultimately, if full understanding is to be achieved, it is important to realize that co-operatives are primarily reflections of local circumstances and of the cultures of their members. This is also true if one wishes to understand Bill Lyall's career and contributions.

This book demonstrates how Lyall developed his leadership skills, knowledge, and understanding while he lived through many of the changes that have dramatically altered Inuit life in the Arctic region during the last sixty years. He spent his early years "on the land", as did most Inuit of his generation. He lived through his family's difficult transition to hamlet life, and he spent much of his later childhood and adolescence in a residential school. This was also a period fraught with challenging experiences. He successfully navigated the immensely difficult task of finding employment in the "new" North, and he also found rewarding work as a member of the Northwest Territories Legislative Assembly and in a variety of organisations. Eventually, he became engaged in his life's work within the developing co-operative movement. Throughout, he has been an astute and engaged observer of all the major trends that have created so many current challenges.

Assessing Bill Lyall's leadership abilities and accomplishments, therefore, means understanding his relationships with Inuit culture and history. It means comprehending his capacity to listen, and to understand what both disturbed and animated the people of his generation and the one that followed. It means recognizing how deeply and accurately he has comprehended the challenges and possibilities confronting the Arctic communities. It requires an understanding of how he reflects the wisdom that the Inuit had gathered from millennia on the land: for example, the need to work together, the limits imposed by a harsh environment, and the need to have the power to be responsible for one's future. From an early age he displayed the wisdom of an elder, a kind of dignified understanding always useful in meeting the tests of everyday life. His background has given him a willingness to express the truth in a direct and concise way, one of the characteristics displayed by the most effective of elders.

Those of us who do not share an indigenous heritage may dismiss the idea of "elder", but we should not. It is a fundamentally important concept among Inuit, because

it honours the wisdom gained through centuries, or even
millennia. In Bill Lyall's case, it meant learning from the
past but not making that knowledge an obstacle to what
the present and future could bring. Rather, the wisdom
gained should encourage serious thoughts about how to
respect the limits of the region as well as its potential for
development; in short, how to use the traditional teachings
of the past as a means of support for what can be learned
and accomplished today. He has consistently argued for an
approach that gives control over development to people of
the North; one that creates employment and opportunity
for those who live there, especially the Inuit; and one that
recognizes that each generation must use natural resources
wisely, in trust, for the ones that follow it—a challenge
of particularly sobering dimensions when taken seriously.

Bill Lyall's perspectives gained through life experience
have enabled him to become a leader because of his
awareness of what was happening within Inuit communities,
and because he could be so easily understood by people he
well understood. When he visited and worked with people
across the Arctic who were trying to use co-ops to help
meet difficult social and economic issues, he immediately
understood and sympathized with them: he had already
"been there," so to speak.

Bill Lyall's work in the context of institutional life also
comes through in his own memoir, and in the chapters
provided by Guy Enoapik, Lucassie Arragutainaq, and
Andy Morrison. These writers demonstrate the challenges
Bill faced in starting and building the Ikaluktutiak
Co-operative in Cambridge Bay. It is a remarkable story
of determined effort and imaginative entrepreneurship in
which Bill played a major role--a story punctuated by the
overcoming of many adversities, struggles that are only
hinted at in the book. Bill does not dwell on such matters
at great length.

More details are provided, however, in the book's
later chapters on the complexities of building Arctic

Co-operatives—a story that suggests the kind of leadership Lyall and others contributed. The people who become involved in co-operatives are generally most drawn to their own local organisations. Building second tier co-operatives is nearly always a challenge, even though people involved with the local co-ops will accept the need for developing them. However, it is a constant struggle to find the resources and to sustain the support necessary for an effective central institution, such as Arctic Co-operatives. The book documents many of these challenges, and it also demonstrates the particular issues that are created or intensified by northern circumstances: explaining the possibilities to local co-ops; enlisting outside support; establishing relationships with the right public servants; securing the most effective place within the developing institutional frameworks of the Arctic territories; training and keeping key personnel; and coping with the costs and complexities of reaching across one third of Canada. The result is a series of useful insights into what is involved in building on local strength to create a greater whole—an approach that holds great promise and possibility in all parts of the country, but perhaps nowhere more importantly than in northern Canada.

There are no simple answers to the question of how such leadership emerged to address so many complex issues, or to why Bill and his colleagues were so successful (though it must be admitted that they made their share of mistakes and errors). In reading through this book, however, it is interesting to try to identify what the secrets of their success were. Many of these secrets may be revealed to readers as they make their way through these pages, but perhaps one will stand out: the stubborn unwillingness to accept defeat. Or, as Bill Lyall puts it in his characteristically simple but thoughtful way: "We only fail when we quit trying." It is an attitude commonly found among the best co-operative leaders, but it takes on a particular relevance in the context of the Arctic co-operatives. And it is also a testimony of how Bill Lyall and his colleagues contributed so much to Canada's most northern co-operatives.

Ian MacPherson[1]
October 2013

---

1. The late Dr. Ian MacPherson was a Professor Emeritus in History and the founding director of the British Columbia Institute for Co-operative Studies at the University of Victoria in Canada.

Acknowledgements

We are very grateful to Bill Lyall for so graciously agreeing to publish his life story. From the beginning, it was a challenge for Bill to find the time for the interview sessions. Although he lives in Cambridge Bay, he travels frequently, as is required by his role as President of Arctic Co-operatives Limited. This book was possible because Bill was willing to squeeze in a few interview hours during some Arctic co-operatives meetings in Winnipeg in early 2011 and, later that spring, during a week-long vacation in Yellowknife.

It was a great privilege to have the opportunity to sit with Bill Lyall for several hours and discuss some pivotal issues concerning the Arctic co-op movement and northern communities in general. The thread of Bill's life is an important one to follow in understanding the recent political and economic transformation of the Canadian Arctic. His vast experience in different levels of leadership and governance in the Canadian North is unique, and his curriculum vitae is impressive: he was an elected Member of the Legislative Assembly of the Northwest Territories; he was vice-chair of the Nunavut Implementation Commission; he was a founding member of the Ikaluktutiak Co-operative, over which he still presides; and he was the President of Canadian Arctic Producers and contributed to its merger with the Canadian Arctic Co-operative Federation to form what is now Arctic Co-operatives Limited. In 2003, Bill was honoured with

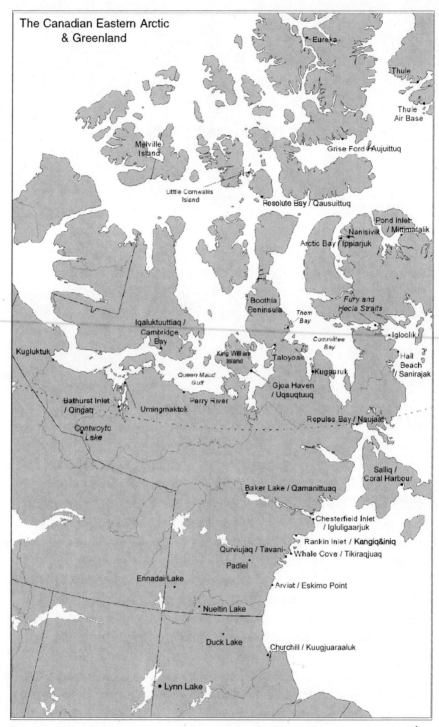

The Canadian Eastern Arctic & Greenland

Eureka

Thule

Thule Air Base

Melville Island

Grise Ford / Aujuittuq

Litttle Cornwallis Island

Resolute Bay / Qausuittuq

Pond Inlet / Mittimatalik

Nanisivik

Arctic Bay / Ippiarjuk

Boothia Peninsula

Fury and Hecla Straits

Thom Bay

Iqaluktuuttiaq / Cambridge Bay

Committee Bay

Igloolik

Kugluktuk

King William Island

Taloyoak

Hall Beach / Sanirajak

Queen Maud Gulf

Kugaaruk

Bathurst Inlet / Qingaq

Umingmaktok

Perry River

Gjoa Haven / Uqsuqtuuq

Contwoyto Lake

Repulse Bay / Naujaat

Salliq / Coral Harbour

Baker Lake / Qamanittuaq

Chesterfield Inlet / Igluligaarjuk

Qurviujaq / Tavani

Rankin Inlet / **Kangiq&iniq**

Whale Cove / Tikiraqjuaq

Padlei

Ennadai Lake

Arviat / Eskimo Point

Nueltin Lake

Duck Lake

Churchill / Kuugjuaraaluk

Lynn Lake

Map design: Mélanie Gagnon, CIÉRA

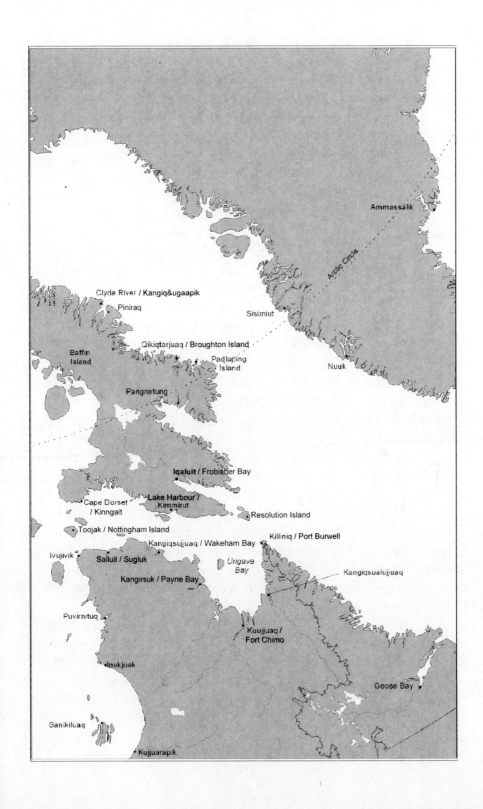

the Order of Canada for his outstanding contribution to the Arctic co-operative movement.

We also express our gratitude to Andy Morrison, Chief Executive Officer of Arctic Co-operatives Limited, who very kindly supported our project from day one and let us interview him about the historical context of the Arctic co-operative movement. Arctic Co-operatives Limited generously invited me to attend their annual general meeting in Winnipeg, which was a precious opportunity to gain an inside experience of the organization. It was also an opportunity to conduct interviews with Lucassie Arragutainaq, President of the Mitiq Co-operative in Sanikiluaq, and Guy Enoapik, a Whale Cove resident and long-time supporter of the co-operative movement in the North. We thank you all for embarking with us on the long process of publishing this book.

It was an honour for our Laval University research team to have Dr. Ian MacPherson writing a foreword for the book. Dr. MacPherson dedicated his professional life to the study of the co-operative movement in Canada. He was the founding director of the British Columbia Institute for Co-operative Studies at the University of Victoria and published extensively on the subject. On November 11, 2013, Dr. MacPherson emailed us the final version of his manuscript. We were astounded and left speechless when informed of his unexpected passing away five days later on November 16. We offer our sincere condolences to his family and friends who were especially numerous in the cooperative movement in Canada and abroad.

Bill's story is part of an ongoing research project at Laval University's CIERA (Centre for Aboriginal Research and Studies). Directed by Professor Frédéric Laugrand, the research project is entitled *Inuit Leadership and Governance in Nunavut and Nunavik: Life Stories, Analytical Perspectives, and Training.* It is funded by the Community University Research Alliance (CURA) program of the Social Sciences and Humanities Research Council of Canada.

We are proud to have the Nunavut Science Institute as the publisher of our *Inuit Leadership and Governance* series, and we appreciated very much Mary Ellen Thomas' enthusiastic response to our partnership request.

The Nunavut Department of Education has been a partner of our CIERA research group for many years and many books. We would especially like to thank Cathy McGregor, Director of Curriculum and School Services for her unfailing support. We sincerely hope that publishing the life stories of prominent Inuit leaders will contribute to the important task of integrating relevant Inuit content into the Nunavut school curriculum.

We also express our sincere gratitude to Professor Laugrand. From the very beginning, he trusted in the value of this project and gave us his full support. We are always and ever thankful to Lise Fortin, CIERA's administrative assistant, who takes such prompt and efficient care of all the administrative matters that truly make a project like this possible. *Merci*, Lise.

Louis McComber
December 2013

Chapter 1

Early Life

My earliest childhood memories are of the Fort Ross area, where I was born in 1941. It was a beautiful place to be. Sea mammals and fish were abundant, and although caribou were few and far between, there were lots of narwhal, white whales, walruses, and seals.[1] I walked a lot with my mother on the land. When the men were out hunting in the summer, the women would go out together and pick heather for the fire and gather roots and berries to eat. They used to walk to the lakes in the spring to go fishing, and in the fall, they would all go out with their children to pick arctic cotton for the *qulliq*.[2] In the spring we would set up camp to dry fish then move again to other places to hunt seal, then again to get berries for the coming winter. That was the cycle we followed every year.

The Inuit name for Fort Ross was Ekegahak. It is right on Bellot Strait, which separates the Boothia Peninsula from Somerset Island.[3] I lived there with my family until 1948. My dad's mother was part Inuk and part German, from the Moravian missionaries in Labrador. His father's family was Scottish and Irish. He grew up in Okak Bay,

---

1. White whales: belugas.
2. A traditional stone lamp used to provide light and heat in the *iglu*.
3. Bellot Strait is a two-kilometre-long strait linking the Gulf of Boothia with Peel Sound. It was named after a French naval officer, Joseph René Bellot, who drowned there in 1852 while on an expedition to search for the lost John Franklin and his men.

which is a little bit north of Nain.[4] My siblings and I are half-and-half, because my mother was a full Inuk.

At the time, there were about fifty or sixty people who camped around the post. James Saittuq's father was there with his family, as well as four or five uncles who were there with their families. But most of the people were from my family, which was originally from Cape Dorset. My grandfather Kavavauk and his family had been moved to Fort Ross by the Hudson's Bay Company (HBC) in 1937.[5] Before that, a group of Inuit from Cape Dorset had been moved to Dundas Harbour and Arctic Bay, where the HBC believed there was good trapping. These Inuit families were moved up there to trap foxes, which is a story that has never been widely reported.[6]

We had no houses, and I don't remember seeing any *qammait*, either.[7] We lived in a tent-frame building, with a little bit of wood and newspaper to cover the walls. They were very harsh living conditions, but the trapping there was

---

4. Bill Lyall's father, Ernie Lyall, was a Hudson's Bay Company trading post manager. Ernie Lyall authored a volume of memoirs entitled *An Arctic Man* (1983). In his memoirs, Ernie Lyall affirms that his father bought a store at Okak Bay, a former Moravian mission (Lyall, 1983: 44, 74).

5. In 1934, the HBC moved 52 Inuit to the High Arctic to open a trading post. In his autobiography, Ernie Lyall reports that they were first moved to Dundas Harbour on Devon Island. Three of the families were from Cape Dorset; they were Kavavouk, Takolik, Inuk and their families *[Ernie Lyall's spelling]*. In 1936, Ernie Lyall was asked by the HBC to close the Dundas Harbour post because of difficulties with sea port access. The three families from Cape Dorset and two from Pond Inlet agreed to be relocated to Arctic Bay, where the HBC re-opened a trading post under the management of Ernie Lyall. The following year, in 1937, the HBC opened a post at Fort Ross. The three Cape Dorset families relocated there along with Emie Lyall, who was by then courting Kavavauk's eldest daughter, Nipisha.

6. Farley Mowat reports this story in his book *The Snow Walker* (1975). His interpretation is harshly criticized by Bill Lyall's father, Ernie Lyall, in his autobiography *An Arctic Man* (Lyall, 1983: 97).

7. A *qammaq* is a winter dwelling built from sod, stones, and skins. The plural form of *qammaq* (or *qarmaq*) is *qammait*.

good. The current in the strait is so swift that it remains ice-free year-round, which guaranteed plenty of sea mammals in the wintertime for the Inuit who were living there.

My dad and grandfather and uncles would go up to the floe edge to hunt seal, which they would shoot with their rifles. In the springtime, when the seal holes were starting to get bigger and seals would come out and lay on the ice, people used to harpoon them as well. They would also bring back a lot of kelp to eat. My father brought that tradition with him from Labrador, where he grew up. Later on in my life I tried seal hunting, but for me it was more a way to have fun than anything else. Things are changing with the newer generations, and seal hunting is slowly fading from our culture.

During the trapping season, we in my father's immediate family lived at Fort Ross by ourselves. The extended family established winter camps in different locations, where they trapped all winter. I remember that Bishop Andrew Atagotaaluk's parents, who had come from Resolute Bay, lived in a steady camp nearby, but my grandfather and the rest of the families moved around to trap.[8]

The children stayed with the women when the men were out hunting. We weren't allowed to stay inside much, the way kids do today, so we played outside year-round. In the winter, we went sliding and travelling with young dogs, and as soon as we were old enough to do chores, we had to learn how to go out to the icebergs and get ice for making tea. When I was about seven years old, I got a .22 calibre rifle to hunt ptarmigan and ducks. I had to learn how to make sure the rifle was in good order.

One of the things we loved to do in the summer was to sit on top of a big hill and watch the narwhals playing in the water off the coast. They were real show-offs. They would swim, dive, and cross tusks, and they swam together,

---

8. Andrew Atagotaaluk was the first Inuit Anglican bishop of the Arctic Diocese.

as if they had been trained by humans. We would also watch the white whales when they were feeding near the bottom. They were beautiful.

World War II was happening during the years we were at Fort Ross, and sometimes we could hear war-time airplanes flying overhead. They were heading for Resolute Bay, which was one of the main relays for airplanes heading overseas. The HBC manager told us we couldn't let them see our lights, so if it was night we would have to black out our windows. The post manager had a two-way radio in his living quarters, powered by a windmill, and my dad and my uncles would listen and talk about what was going on overseas.

Inuktitut was the only language spoken at Fort Ross, so my father had to explain to everyone what the war was all about. The Inuit there didn't know much about the Germans or why these countries were fighting. In fact, they didn't know much about the outside world at all. When they found out the war had ended, my grandfather and the men were at our fishing camp.[9] I remember there was still ice on the sea and it was a beautiful day. An airplane dropped the mail, and soon after that we heard my dad and everybody else talking about how the war was over.

I also remember a medical emergency that took place when we lived in Fort Ross. My dad and my uncle had to go to a nearby camp to pick up David Kaomeyok, who was seriously ill, and they brought him back in a box on their sled.[10] His mother had already amputated one of his legs. An armed forces airplane came from Pond Inlet and took him away. My dad tells this story in his book. Another time, an airplane crashed in Fort Ross.[11] Fortunately, nobody got hurt and a second airplane came and picked up the crew.

9. German forces surrendered officially on May 8, 1945. Japan sur-
    rendered on August 15, 1945.
10. See: Lyall, 160-165. Ernie Lyall spells the name as "Kaymayook".
11. A DC3 bringing supplies to Fort Ross crashed in February 1949. The
    HBC had already closed its trading post there and supplies were low
    for the remaining families still living in the area. Luckily, there were
    no casualties. (Lyall, 162-163)

Sarah Nipisha Lyall, holding Dennis Lyall, in Taloyoak, 1951.
Photo credit: Richard Harrington, Library Archives Canada PA-147200

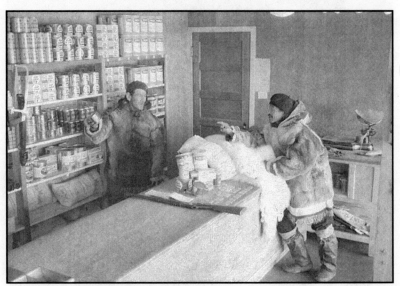

**Ernie Lyall and unidentified man, in the Hudson's Bay
Company store in Taloyoak, formerly Spence Bay, in 1951.**
Photo credit: Richard Harrington, Library and Archives Canada.
PA-147198.

The R.M.S. Nascopie, anchored in Pangnirtung Fiord.
Photo credit: George Hunter/National Film Board of Canada, Library and
Archives Canada.

**Bella Lyall Wilcox, carrying her sister Betty Lyall Brewster
in her amauti, in Taloyoak, then called Spence Bay.
Circa 1961.**
Photo credit: Health and Welfare Canada collection/Library
and Archives Canada / e004665165.

Eventually, the HBC decided that the Fort Ross trading post had to be moved to a better place, where the shipping route would be more reliable. The HBC supply ship, the *Nascopie*, hadn't been able to get into Fort Ross for two years in a row, meaning that yearly supplies couldn't be delivered.[12] My dad and one of my uncles travelled around with people from the HBC to find a new location. Taloyoak was the place they decided on, although at the time they called it "Taloyaoit", which means "place of the caribou blinds".[13]

I was seven years old when the post was moved, in the spring of 1948. One building was pulled by dog team from Fort Ross to Taloyoak, about 210 kilometres south. It was the generator house for the HBC, and it took about a month to move. I moved with my parents and my sisters Bella, Barbara, and Betty. My other siblings were born in Spence Bay later on. My grandfather and his immediate family stayed on at Fort Ross for a while and then joined us a couple of years later. My older brother Johnny stayed with them in Fort Ross, because in an Inuit family, the daughters always leave one of their sons to stay with the grandparents.

My father knew a lot of the Netsilingmiut who were already living in the Spence Bay area.[14] He used to travel back and forth to meet ships that traded in the region, such

12. The *Nascopie* grounded on a reef and eventually sank near Cape Dorset in 1947.
13. The Canadian government called the settlement Spence Bay until 1992, when the name reverted to Taloyoak. Bill uses the names interchangeably.
14. The Netsilik Inuit were the last group of Canadian Inuit to be contacted by missionaries. They lived in the area of Committee Bay, Victoria Strait, and Summerset Island. Today Netsilingmiut are concentrated in the communities of Kugaaruk, Taloyoak, and Gjoa Haven. In the 1960s the National Film Board of Canada produced a remarkable series of films on the Netsilik traditional way of life, *The Netsilik Eskimo* (1967).

as the Klengenberg ship sailing from Aklavik.[15] He knew
Pialak, Anaija, and Iqualak and their families. Once the
trading post was set up, people came to trade there from
Pelly Bay, Back River, and Gjoa Haven.[16] Most of them
were living at Back River.

Fishing is very good in that part of the Central Arctic,
south of Resolute Bay and around Taloyoak, Kugaaruk,
and Cambridge Bay. The mainstay there is fish. Instead
of carrying seal meat in the back of their dog sleds for dog
food, the people there used to carry big trouts instead.
Today I run a fish camp in the region, and a lot of the
places I take people to have been studied by archaeologists.
People have been living and fishing there for 3,000 years.

In Spence Bay, I lived with my parents in a wooden
house with an oil stove. That was something different for
us. I remember being behind the counter of the trading
post with my father. If somebody wanted flour, my siblings
or I would get it and put it on the table.

We had never spoken English in Fort Ross, but I
started to pick it up when we moved to Spence Bay, where
English-speaking missionaries, RCMP officers, and HBC
people were beginning to settle. The Roman Catholics
were travelling into Spence Bay from Gjoa Haven and
Pelly Bay by dog team, and they and the Anglicans later
built missions there.

15. Christian Klengenberg was a Danish whaler and trader known to the
    Inuit as Charliuyak . In 1916, Klengenberg established the first trading
    posts in the Kitikmeot region. See: http://www.kitikmeotheritage.
    ca/Angulalk/whaler/klenberg.htm and http://en.wikipedia.org/wiki/
    Christian_Klengenberg. Christian's son, Patsy Klengenberg, became
    captain of the HBC ship *Aklavik*, which he purchased in 1942. See:
    http://www.kitikmeotheritage.ca/Angulalk/whaler/patsy/patsy.htm
16. Gjoa Haven is known as Uqsuqtuuq in Inuktitut. Pelly Bay is now
    called Kugaaruk.

Chapter 2

Being Educated
to Forget Inuktitut

There was no school in Spence Bay when I was a boy, so in 1950 I was sent to Aklavik to get an education.[1] We grew up hearing about the importance of school, and even though it was very hard to leave my family, my dad expected me to go out and better myself. When we went away to school, we really missed our families. As a boy, though, I put on a brave front and didn't admit that I missed home. The world was changing, and we were expected to go to school to get ready for it. By that time, the government was already pushing people into the settlements so that it could deliver services more efficiently.

Four of us left Spence Bay together: my older sister Bella; my younger sister Barbara; a girl named Peggy Iqaluuk, who was Iqualaq's step daughter; and me. We were put on a Canso airplane, which the HBC had bought from the armed forces after the war.[2] We flew from Spence

---

1. The first school in Spence Bay was built in 1959. In Aklavik the Anglican school, established in 1936, was called All Saints Residential School.
2. The Canadian-built PBY Catalina was known in Canada as the Canso, a "flying boat" used widely during World War II. The Canso is still used today in firefighting operations.

Bay to Cambridge Bay, and from there we sailed on the HBC supply ship *Fort Hearne* to Tuktoyaktuk.

In Cambridge Bay we were joined by three or four other young people travelling to Aklavik to go to school. Our chaperone for the trip from Cambridge Bay to Tuktoyaktuk was an Anglican minister from Coppermine, Archdeacon Webster. In Tuktoyaktuk, some of our group stayed with a teacher, but Peter Atighioyak, from Cambridge Bay, and I stayed with Reverend Thomas Umauk. He was an Inuvialuit Anglican minister. He served us some traditional Inuvialuit food on the floor: *muktuk*, dried meat, and dry fish. We all sat down on the floor to eat, but because I looked like a white kid, Thomas Umauq opened a can of meat for me. I thought it was a special treat, because we never ate that at home, and when I finished it I started to eat the *muktuk* and the dried meat as well. He must have been surprised to see that!

We waited in Tuktoyaktuk for the mission boat from Aklavik to come and get us. The Anglican Church had two boats: the *Messenger* was a river boat that picked up kids from Tuktoyaktuk, and the *Beacon* was a scow that picked up kids upriver, from Fort McPherson and Arctic Red River. I was part of the group that went on the *Messenger*.

We stopped at camps along the Mackenzie River for other kids who were going to the residential school hostel. The first batch of kids we picked up was from Buster Kailek's family. He was a reindeer herder from the Central Arctic, and it was the first time his kids were going away to school, too. Bob and George Kailek both later became very good friends of mine.

After we arrived in Aklavik, the truth hit home: we were going to be living with complete strangers and everything was going to be in English. We quickly saw that if we spoke Inuktitut we would be punished for it, even if it was outdoors in the schoolyard. That was when I understood that I had truly left behind my family and all that I knew behind. Everything was so different: the food, the language, the people, and even the houses. Everybody in Aklavik lived in houses; nobody lived in tents, even in the summer.

Essentially, I grew up at that residential school. I wasn't able to return home for seven years. Those of us from Spence Bay, Cambridge Bay, and Sachs Harbour had to stay at the hostel year round, because it was too far to go back home during the holidays, and the mission boats only went as far as Tuktoyaktuk or up the river to Fort McPherson. Once in a while we would receive letters from home, and I would also get radio messages from my dad, through a family friend in the armed forces in Aklavik who had a ham radio.

The All Saints Residential School in Aklavik.
Photo credit: Anglican General Synods Archives P75-103-57-83

Apart from the crew of the odd small airplane, the only white people I had ever seen were the HBC managers, RCMP officers, and missionaries. Tuktoyaktuk was an Eskimo community, Fort McPherson was an Indian community, and Aklavik, then the administrative centre of the region, was mixed. Up to that point, I had never seen anybody fight in my life, and I had never seen a drunken person, but I saw it all when I got to Aklavik. I learned to defend myself right away!

There had always been a lot of hostility between Indian and Inuit children, yet in the student hostel we were all put together. The Eskimo kids didn't really talk to me, because I looked like a white kid, and the Indian kids thought I was a white Eskimo. Caught in between, I befriended both Indian guys and Eskimo guys and learned to fight. I started boxing and joined the Cubs and, later, the Scouts. The people I met there became very good friends for life, whether they were Indian or Inuvialuit.

We had to learn English pretty quickly. The only time we heard Inuktitut was if we went to the Eskimo church service on Sunday. I went to every one of them. I joined the choir, and I used to love the ten-minute walk to the church. At home we didn't have to pray every morning, but at school we had to pray morning, noon, and evening. One of the difficult things for me about being at the school was that my two sisters were on the other side of the building, but I couldn't talk to them. The church was the only place where we could visit each other and talk a little bit without sneaking around to do it.

Life at the school was all about discipline, both institutionally and personally. We knew we were there to learn. We boys would compete to see who could do better than the next at reading, writing, and arithmetic. We competed to see who could do the best or fastest job of cleaning the gymnasium or cleaning the slop buckets or washing dishes in the dining room. On weekends, we used to make pies and bread. That was a competition, too, to see who could make the best bread and buns.

The only time I ever missed school was if I was sick. Of course, in a residential school when one person got sick, the illness usually ran through the whole hostel, where three to four hundred kids ate and slept together. Everything was run by the clock, with very strict hours: we would wake up early, pray, do some chores, eat breakfast, do a few more chores, then be in class at nine o'clock. We did that every day. We would be assigned one classroom and one teacher, who taught us all the subjects. The classrooms were in the same building, so there weren't many ways to stay out of class without anyone knowing. In fact, another reason I joined the choir was so I could get away from the hostel for a while every week!

One of the things about living at the Anglican hostel is that we missed out on family life. We did not receive any parenting when we were there. Parenting can only be taught within a family, and we didn't get that. When we started earning wages and having children, we didn't really have the skills to raise our children properly. I have four children with my present wife; it is hard for them to leave home and live their own lives. They want to stay in our community, but there are no jobs here for them here. A lot of our people are like that.

Despite all that, Aklavik was a good learning experience for me. I had a lot of good times and good friends there. At the hostel we had a garden, where we planted potatoes, carrots, and cabbage. There were Cubs and Boy Scouts, and when school was over in the summer I had work digging ditches for the town of Aklavik. Sometimes I chopped wood for people, and I got my learner's permit to drive a tractor so I could get work unloading the supply ships. I would make around nine dollars a day transporting all the freight for the school, the hostel, and the hospital.

Our teenage years in Aklavik were good. I appreciate the education that I received while I was there. Our people got short shrift on a lot of things, including being exposed to sexual abuse at some of those schools, but I didn't see any of that during the time I was at the Anglican hostel. Some people have had a hard time putting their residential school experiences behind them, but I decided to close that door. It is in the past.

In 1957, after I finished grade nine, my younger sister Barbara and I finally returned home to see our family. My older sister had already gone back because she couldn't cope

with being away. Barbara and I went over to Inuvik on a
Cessna 185 plane, where my dad got us a ride on the ship,
the *Fort Hearne*. In return for the passage, my sister and I
worked in the kitchen on board, for my dad's friend Captain
Thomas. We sailed for Cambridge Bay and spent four or
five days in 25-foot-high waves. I stayed in the HBC purser's
bedroom, and my sister stayed in the captain's quarters. She
didn't get seasick, but my head was out of the porthole for
the whole trip! My older sister Bella was in Cambridge Bay,
working at the nursing station, so we stayed with her while
we waited for the RCMP's annual trip into the settlements.

The RCMP was flying three airplanes in those days:
a Grumman Goose, a Beaver, and a Single Otter.[3] They
would fly from Yellowknife up into the Central Arctic—
Coppermine, Cambridge, Taloyoak,—where the head of
the RCMP would go in to inspect the RCMP posts. For
the trip home, I sat in the right-hand seat of the Otter. The
plane was carrying all the freight and luggage for the RCMP
posts. When we got to Spence Bay, we couldn't land in the
bay because of the high winds, so we set down behind the
RCMP water reservoir. All the people in the community
were there for our arrival.

I hadn't seen my mom and dad for seven years. When
my sister and I got off the plane, it was a joyful but very
painful moment. I was finally home, yet when I saw my
mother we couldn't even communicate with each other.
We kids had been made to forget Inuktitut; I couldn't
speak my own language anymore. I couldn't speak to my
mother, and she couldn't speak to me, so we just cried. It
was very hard for us. To this day, I still haven't gotten my
Inuktitut completely back. It was like that for a lot of us.

After my visit home, I brought my other brother, Pat,
back to Aklavik for school. We left Taloyoak and went
to Cambridge Bay, where we were supposed to take the

---

3. The Grumman Goose was an amphibious aircraft used extensively
during World War II.

Hudson's Bay Company's supply ship *Netsilik* onward. Instead, my dad arranged for us to take a DEW Line plane from Cambridge Bay to Tuktoyaktuk.[4] That was a lucky break, because the *Netsilik* went aground in a big storm on its way back to Tuktoyaktuk!

Back in Aklavik, the superintendent of schools, Mr. Holman, told me that my studies there were completed and that I could return home for good. I told him there was nothing for me at home anymore, and so he suggested I go to the new high school in Yellowknife that went up to grade 12. It had both academics and a trade school, with automotive mechanics, welding, and carpentry. I told him I wanted to go there.

In Yellowknife I decided to study automotive mechanics. If I could do it over, I would choose a different program, but back then I wanted to get a trade so I could make a living and get ahead in life. I took academic studies part-time and trades part-time. I worked in auto shops after school and for summer jobs, but I didn't get any trade papers at the end of my schooling because there were no apprenticeship programs in the Northwest Territories at that time.

I told the superintendent, Mr. Boxer, that I wanted certification and asked him what the next step was.[5] He told me I'd have to go down to Alberta to apprentice in whatever I wanted to do. The problem was that I couldn't go to school in Alberta unless I had an academic grade 10 and could pass an entrance exam for their program. I went to Inuvik for a year to get my grade 10 and stayed at the hostel there for another year, at Stringer Hall.[6]

---

4. The DEW Line, the Distant Early Warning radar network, was constructed all across the Arctic beginning in 1955.
5. Albert (Bert) Boxer was superintendent at Akaitcho Hall in Yellowknife.
6. Stringer Hall was the Anglican hostel in Inuvik. It had the capacity to accommodate 250 students.

After that, I went to Alberta and began a four-year program to study as an apprentice automotive mechanic. I married my first wife there and we had two sons. In 1968, in my third year of training, I returned to Spence Bay to see my parents for Christmas. I didn't have enough money to buy a plane ticket to go back to Alberta and got stuck in Cambridge Bay on my way back. I stayed on there and eventually went to work at the power house for the Northern Canada Power Commission (NCPC). Later, I started a taxi company and got involved with the co-op. And today, I'm still broke!

Chapter 3

The Cambridge Bay
Fishery Co-operative

I worked in Cambridge Bay for about a year before I met my present wife, Jessie. Together we have four children: two boys and two girls. From them, we have thirteen grandchildren and one great-grandson. Including my two oldest children's families, I have seventeen grandchildren all together.

It was a good place to live. I always talk about Cambridge Bay as I know it, as a bastardized town. The people came in from camps on the land as far west as Tuktoyaktuk, from Pelly Bay in the east, and from Gjoa Haven and Spence Bay. As far as I could see, there was never any bad blood between these groups of people.[1] They understood that the government was bringing them into settlements in order to better look after the Arctic population. Cambridge Bay was chosen as a place to set up services because the DEW Line site infrastructure was already there.[2] It was also a good harbour and there was already an Inuit summer camp there. There were quite a few other camps in the area, all of them about forty to sixty miles apart from each other. They were

1. Spence Bay has been called Taloyoak since 1992. It is located on the Boothia Peninsula. Pelly Bay has been called Kugaaruk since 1999 and is located on the east side of the Gulf of Boothia.
2. A DEW Line Station was established in Cambridge Bay in 1957. The station is still in operation as Cam-Main, of the current North Warning System.

across the strait, in the Coronation Gulf, on Perry Island, at Bathurst Inlet, and at Bay Chimo. The government wanted to centralize people into settlements to look after them better. That is what they explained at that time. Everybody realized that together, life would be easier to manage. At the same time, people were being taken out of camps to be sent to tuberculosis hospitals, and children were sent to residential schools.

When I first arrived in Cambridge Bay, I drove a sewage truck, a water truck, and a fuel truck, but my interests were not really there. When a good job came up with NCPC, I applied and I worked there for five years.[3] As a powerhouse operator, I worked eight-hour shifts watching all the gauges, doing mechanical maintenance on the engines, and installing power lines.

The meat processing plant, Cambridge Bay
[Photo taken by Tessa Macintosh]
Photo credit: NWT Archives/Northwest Territories. Dept. of Public Works and Services fonds/G-1995-001: 4902

---

3. NCPC: The Northern Canada Power Commission changed its name, in 1989, to the Northwest Territories Power Corporation.

I was glad to see that the people in Cambridge Bay were running an Arctic char fishery co-operative. Back in Aklavik, I had started to get interested in co-ops when I read a social studies book about how the co-op movement started, what it was doing, and the people who started it. And when I was at trade school in Alberta, I became familiar with the co-op in Wetaskiwin. Co-operatives reminded me so much of the way we Inuit used to live, such as the way my family did in Fort Ross. Then, when I returned to the North in the late 1960s, I realized that our people had already started some co-operatives.

I started to get involved with the co-op as soon as I got there, although my full-time involvement came later on. Now we run a lot of operations, but back then we were just a commercial fishing co-operative. The federal government had developed the Cambridge Bay fishery in 1961 as an experimental venture. Initially, it was a semi-government operation, but we bought it out in 1977 and started our own administration using our own methods. It was important that we no longer rely on the government, so we ran it on our own. We tried to do things a little bit differently.

In the beginning, the government fishery had been a competitive free-for-all, with some individuals catching their quota very quickly and some not. We did it differently. If six people went out to a river, they all agreed to work together and they all agreed to split the money as a team. I remember being out in the fish camp, when the fish were fully running; I'd go to bed at four o'clock in the morning and get up at seven to go pull my nets. Sometimes I would do that for a few days in a row. We would get very tired, but it was a good source of fast income that would give us a chance to buy a new snowmobile or an outboard motor. It still operates that way today, with all the people working in the rivers splitting the money at the end.

When I was working for the NCPC, I would use my summer holidays to fish for the co-op. The commercial fishery generally started in early July or early August and it went until the end of August. I used to go to the nearest fishing camp, which was 40 miles away. Even later on, when I became Member of the Northwest Territories Legislative Assembly for the Central Arctic in 1975, I kept fishing with the members of the co-operative.

I always took my family out there for the duration of the fishing season. My wife did a lot of work with the fishermen who were there. She was a teacher, and she didn't want to interfere with the work of the other people at the fish processing plant in town, so she would come out and work with me. It was also a chance to get our kids out on the land. When they were younger, they enjoyed it. It is a very short season, but it is very hard work. Today, my hands show that I have been working in cold water for years and years!

Every year, before the commercial fishing season began, we would have to make sure that we were going to get a good enough price for the fish we caught. We always sold our fish to the Freshwater Fish Marketing Corporation in Winnipeg, a company that the co-operative had been dealing with from the beginning. We had a quota for 209,000 pounds of fish that could be caught out of six or seven rivers. Back then, transporting fresh fish by airplane was viable within a 100 mile radius of Cambridge Bay, but with rises in transportation costs that isn't the case anymore. Today, they're not fishing two of the rivers that we used to fish, because it's not really viable to go that far. People still catch fish from Ellis River, one of the outlying rivers, but the fish is only sold locally.

After we negotiated with the wholesaler, we would lease an airplane for the summer to transport the catch. The best airplane for our use was always the Beaver, but over the years we worked with many airlines that flew our fish in Single Otters, Twin Otters, and at one point, a Cessna 185.[4,5]

---

4. The De Havilland Beaver is a bush plane that can be equipped with floats or skis.
5. The De Havilland Canada DHC-3 Otter and the DHC-6 Twin Otter are both STOL (short take-off and landing) aircraft of the kind still widely used in the Canadian Arctic.

We would launch the spring fishery when the char started to come downriver, around the beginning of July. That's when the ocean, lakes, and rivers would open up. You have to be very careful in managing all the elements of a fishery. You're fighting the weather all the time. In the Arctic, char come up the river at the windiest time of the year, when there is a lot of heavy fog, too. The weather can be a problem for the aircraft that transport the fish back to Cambridge Bay. We use commercial traps, although in the river where I used to fish, we couldn't use those because the river was too fast and deep.

We would fish for a couple of weeks and catch enough to get the processing going, and then we would go back for the second part of our season, from mid-August until we were done, usually in early September. If our wives didn't go out to the commercial fishery, they stayed in town to do processing at the fish plant. After the plane brought the fish to town, it was taken to the plant to be washed, cleaned, hung, and blast-frozen. We would employ about thirty fishermen and maybe forty local women, men, and kids from the school. It was quite an operation, but unfortunately it was only seasonal.

The fishery operation is still running today, but it is now managed by the Nunavut Development Corporation.[6] That means it is once again a semi-governmental operation. We are now competing with farmed char, which tastes like paper to me. Our fish, whether frozen or fresh, is completely natural. The Arctic char is a fragile fish because it lives in very cold water. You can't just keep it on ice for a day or two, or the meat will start to get soft. That is why we catch it and blast-freeze it within ten hours. We used to sell the fish gutted and de-gilled, frozen whole and packaged into seventy-five pound crates. There were

---

6. Nunavut Development Corporation is a territorial government agency that invests in local businesses in Nunavut communities. See: http://www.ndcorp.nu.ca

two to four-pound packages, then five to seven pounds, eight to ten, and ten pounds and over. Nowadays some secondary processing is done right here in Cambridge Bay. They still sell whole fish, but they also sell headless and tailless fish, fillets, cold- and hot-smoked fish, and canned char chowder.

Developing the Cambridge Bay Co-operative

When I arrived in Cambridge Bay, there were already other co-operatives operating in the North—in Pelly Bay and in Cape Dorset. In the beginning, northern co-ops were government programs that were, perhaps, not expected to work. They did work, though, because they are based on a model that makes sense to us. I always preach that we need co-operatives because that is the way the Inuit people live, up here in this harsh country. The case is the same for First Nations people as well. Before the white man came, if one day I couldn't find food, and I knew you were two hundred miles away from me, I could go visit you and you would provide me with food. Without the simple notion that helping each other makes life easier and better, we wouldn't be up here today.

The whole Cambridge Bay co-op started around that fishery, and as advisors started coming in and showing us the way co-ops work down South, we began to expand. Andrew Goussaert was a driving force behind those co-op expansions.[7] At around the same time, the government was offering what they called "winter work programs" so people could have work. My own involvement in the co-op became more significant after 1975, when I won a seat in the Northwest Territories Legislative Assembly for the first

---

7. Andrew Goussaert was a former Roman Catholic missionary of the Order of the Oblates of Mary Immaculate and a pivotal actor in the development of the co-operative movement in the Arctic. He later became the president of the Canadian Arctic Co-operative Federation Limited.

time. As an MLA, whenever I returned to Cambridge Bay from the legislature in Yellowknife, I would have nothing to do with my time. I started working with the co-op, volunteering my time, to do something in between sessions. My big commitment was to start up our own grocery store as a way to improve services in our community. I eventually ran for the position of co-op director.

We started to produce handicrafts, with a ladies' sewing centre, and we had a little transient centre where people could stay when they came to the settlement. That started off with about seven beds, and eventually we brought in a cook. In the late 1970s we started a real hotel, which later expanded into a twenty-bed facility.

In 1981, we got together and built the grocery store. There were already some co-op stores in Pelly Bay, Spence Bay, and Gjoa Haven, but this was Cambridge Bay's first. The building is still there, being used as a warehouse. We built it from scrap material, and it is the best building in town for holding heat. The first year we ran the grocery store, it was cash-only. We built up a capital of $1 million dollars in the first year. Before that we would have to go to the banks to borrow money for start-up projects, and then all of a sudden we had our own money to put to use. After we built an addition onto the hotel, the banks were coming to us, offering to lend us money! Since then we have built a new store and a new warehouse, which is attached to the store.

Ten years later, we were operating a cable company, selling gasoline, and running a taxi service. When I decided to let my own taxi business go, I signed the licence over to the co-operative and we started bidding for government mail runs from the airport and for intergovernmental deliveries. We sorted and delivered the mail for about seven government buildings. Eventually we tried to get out of the taxi business, because by then we had two private taxi services in the community. Our co-op members wanted to have some kind of transportation to bring their shopping home, though, and we felt that we couldn't cut that service. My view is that since our losses aren't that great, and as long as we make money in other places, we should keep the taxi so that elders can get rides home.

In the meantime, we started putting money together to build a new store, and we bought another hotel. We bought the new one so we could shut the old one down, but since the climate here requires that we keep buildings heated year-round, we have continued to use it for overflow. A new science centre is being built in Cambridge Bay, and we're thinking about demolishing the old hotel and building self-contained housing units for transient people to rent.[8]

---

8. The new Canada High Arctic Research Station, CHARS, will cost $142.5 million and should be completed in 2017.

Chapter 4

Running for Office

In the early 1970s, I got involved with the first Cambridge Bay settlement council. We had an education committee and a social services committee—all kinds of committees to get things organized and working. I went to a lot of land claims meetings and helped with our local Inuit associations. I tried to get information about what they needed and I was involved in taking inventories of wildlife. At the same time, I was managing the co-operative and trying to find the best ways to bring useful services to the community. I did all those things because I felt I had to.

While I was chair of the settlement council, I became a sort of instructor on settlement organization for the territorial government. It wasn't a full-time job, but I was travelling so much that I had to quit my job at the power plant. I chose to work for the people instead of the power corporation. I could have gone a long way with the NCPC, but my father taught his kids that we are here to help our fellow man. All of my brothers were very involved in political life and did a lot of work with organizations and with setting up hamlet councils. My mother was also very much involved in the land claims process and attended a lot of land claims meetings.

My oldest brother, Johnny, was a special constable with the Royal Canadian Mounted Police in Cambridge Bay for twenty-two years. He eventually left for a posting in

Iqaluit. My other brother Pat flew in and out of Cambridge Bay, working for the DEW Line. My older sister Bella came in to live there too, a little later. My other brother worked with me for a while at the power plant, and we built the new power plant as well. We put up some lines, on our own, for the power company. Many local people worked on it too.

In 1975, I ran for the Northwest Territories Council elections. It was the first fully elected council in the Northwest Territories.[1] As a young and energetic man, I thought being on the territorial council would help my region and our people, but I learned a quick, hard lesson. Within a few months I realized that the government already had a five-year plan, a ten-year plan, as well as fifteen- and twenty-year plans for all the settlements. That affected us in the Central Arctic in a lot of ways. You couldn't fast-track any important requests for new equipment, for example, because the territorial council had already planned out all future equipment purchases.

I sat on every legislative assembly committee I could. I chaired the legislative Committee of the Whole so I could be involved in all the new legislation that was drafted on wildlife and education. It was important to speak up for the communities we represented. A centrally located place like Cambridge Bay got more equipment than smaller settlements like Gjoa Haven, Pelly Bay, or Spence Bay. They didn't even have proper water trucks; they were

1. From 1905, the Northwest Territories was administered by a commissioner who was supported by an advisory council. The first aboriginal representative on this council was Abraham Okpik, who was appointed in 1965. In 1975, for the first time, all members of the Northwest Territories Legislative Council were elected. This was a result of the recommendations of the Advisory Commission on the Development of Government in the Northwest Territories, better known as the Carrother's Commission. In 1976 the Northwest Territories Legislative Council changed its name to the Legislative Assembly of the Northwest Territories.

still using water tanks pulled by tractors. If we asked for a new fire truck, they would tell us to use the water truck. I contributed to getting that changed. If people in those smaller settlements were expected to work properly, they needed to have the proper machinery. Some of the equipment got fast-tracked after that, because somebody living right there in the region was telling the government what was needed. I thought that the smaller settlements should have equal access to the kinds of services that everybody else had.

Another thing I worked on was a policy on the use of government vehicles. At one point we started to realize that the territorial government employees in Cambridge Bay were using government trucks and snowmobiles after working hours. People didn't like to see them using government vehicles for personal use. I thought that ought to change, and I got it changed. After that, if a government employee needed a boat, snowmobile, or four-wheeler for their job, they had to get somebody who had one in the community and pay for the rental. The government employees eventually managed to do their work that way.

When I was an MLA, the people of Holman Island held a plebiscite and decided to be part of Nunavut when that new territory would be formed. Nellie Cournoyea said the plebiscite was not done correctly, so they organized a new one; and then the vote went the other way. Holman Island is now part of the Northwest Territories.[2] Nellie Cournoyea was instrumental in a lot of decisions made by the government of the Northwest Territories. She is a very

2. Nellie Cournoyea was Premier of the Northwest Territories from 1991 to 1995. She is now the chief executive officer and chair of the Inuvialuit Regional Corporation. All together, Nellie Cournoyea served 17 years as Member of the Northwest Territories Legislative Assembly. She was the founding chair of the Aboriginal Pipeline Group and is now a director within that organization.

strong person, and a lot of the things that the Western
Arctic now has were gotten because of Nellie.

As an MLA, I made $8,000 a year. I had a travel
budget of $3,000, which means that if I were to charter
a plane to go to see my constituents at Bay Chimo, my
whole budget would have been used up. Instead, I used to
jump on government charters and visit my constituency
that way. I used to go in once before the legislative session
started and again after the session. The government
departments were just being formed, and the territorial
government staff was starting to visit the communities.
Social workers were being brought in, and the government
was training people to run their own settlements. That is
when centralization began to happen, when they began
pulling everybody off the land.

I was pretty good friends with Stuart Hodgson,
Commissioner of the NWT, so every time he came out
our way he would ask me if I needed a ride anywhere.[3] He
did that for a lot of other people too. He always travelled
with his assistant Rod Morrison, and when we would be
coming in to land in a settlement, Stu would say, "Hey,
Rod, what did I promise these guys?" Rod would fill him
in before he got there, and then at the local community
meeting, Stu would say, "Yes, that will be on the barge
for you!"

When the whole Northwest Territories government
moved to Yellowknife, the federal government had given

---

3. Stuart (Stu) Milton Hodgson was Commissioner of the Northwest
   Territories from 1967 to 1979. Following the report of A. W. R.
   Carrothers on the development of political institutions in the NWT,
   Stu Hodgson was given the task of developing a representative
   government for the territories. That region covered what is now
   the NWT and Nunavut. When Hodgson and his staff moved to
   Yellowknife in 1967, the NWT Council was only a consultative body.
   By the time he left in 1979, he had put in place an elected government.
   Unlike Canada's provinces, fully elected territorial governments are
   still under the jurisdiction of the Minister of Aboriginal Affairs and
   Northern Development Canada.

Stu an open chequebook. He made all the decisions by himself. The Northwest Territories Council was just an advisory council, and most members were appointed. When a real government was formed, all the members of the legislative assembly had to be elected. Even then, with the fixed long-range plans, our decision-making powers were still pretty limited. Sometimes elected officials declare, "I did that—I got that new school built for our community!" They didn't, of course, because all those infrastructure plans were already in place.

Inuit in the Eastern Arctic had it even harder back then. I could see their MLA, Bryan Pearson, struggling against the western territories.[4] The capital was in Yellowknife, and the closest settlements got whatever they needed. Bryan was crying in the wilderness, trying to do something for his people in the East, but he didn't get much help. In the Central Arctic we were lucky; we got fairly good support from Yellowknife because we were closer to it. Today, things are reversed: Iqaluit is the capital of Nunavut, and the western part of the territory feels left out. In western Nunavut, though, we have always been pretty self-reliant. We always manage to do what we need to do.

As a young man in Alberta in the late '60s and early '70s, I saw people in southern Canada become more aggressive in trying to get their rights recognized. I often thought, then, that if that could happen south of us, it should be happening in the North as well. The Inuit Tapirisat of Canada land claims negotiations were very important to me at that time—I hadn't run for the territorial council solely to help the people in Cambridge Bay or Taloyoak; I ran to help build the Northwest

---

4. Bryan Pearson was elected as MLA for the district of the Eastern Arctic in 1970. He replaced Simonie Michael, who was the first elected Inuk to sit at the territorial council. In 1975, Pearson was re-elected in the district of South Baffin.

Territories.[5] I went on to become one of the Nunavut Implementation Commissioners, and I co-chaired that commission with John Amagoalik.[6]

5. Inuit Tapirisat of Canada was created in 1971 as an offspring of the Indian-Eskimo Association. In 1976, it engaged in land claims negotiations with the federal government by presenting its first proposition for the creation of Nunavut in a working paper entitled *Nunavut: A Proposal for the Settlement of Inuit Lands in the Northwest Territories*. In 2001 the organization changed names and is now known as Inuit Tapiriit Kanatami.
6. The Nunavut Implementation Commission (NIC) was created in 1993 as a result of the signing of the Nunavut Land Claims Agreement. It was composed of nine commissioners appointed by the federal government, the Government of the Northwest Territories, and Nunavut Tunngavik Inc. Chaired by John Amagoalik, the NIC had the mandate to design the structure of the new Nunavut government.

Chapter 5

Living with Co-operatives

Bill Lyall, at the Canadian Co-operative Achievement Awards.
Photo credit: Arctic Co-operatives Limited

Cooperation is the basis of Inuit life: we help ourselves by helping each other. The seven principles of the co-operative movement are all related to how Inuit work together.[1] In fact, there were only six principles adhered to

---

1. The principles: voluntary and open membership; democratic member control; member economic participation; autonomy and independence; education, training and information; cooperation among co-operatives; and concern for community. See: http://www.ica.coop/coop/principles. html.

by the Canadian Co-operative Association until 1995, when Dr. Ian MacPherson and a team of experts were commissioned to look into them to see if we were still meeting the six criteria.[2] As a co-operative movement in northern Canada, we at Arctic Co-operatives Limited suggested that there was something missing. We thought that caring for our communities ought to be a central feature. They made that the seventh principle of the Canadian co-operative movement.

In the spirit of caring for our community, we never say "no" to the schools when they ask for a donation. For example, we've distributed apples to all the students, and we have a special budget to sponsor special events at the school. In our hamlet, when somebody passes on we take a hamper of food over to the family, because we know that the whole community is going to be visiting. We make sure that they'll have food and tea to share with their family and friends.

Community members feel a very strong sense of ownership in our co-op. For elders who were here before the monetary system was introduced to the North, it can be hard to understand that we have to operate as a business. They say, "It's my co-operative! I'm a member. If I co-own the grocery store, why can't I just take a loaf of bread home without paying for it?" We have to explain that if everybody took a loaf of bread home, we'd be out of business.

On the other hand, some people are against co-operatives. I've heard politicians joking that the Communist Party of Canada was based in the North! Of course that is far from the truth, because in communism, the state controls everything and redistributes everything. In a co-operative,

---

2. Ian MacPherson was the founder of the British Colombia Institute for Co-operatives Studies (BCICS) and the founder and president of the Canadian Co-operative Association. McPherson was part of a team who ran consultations and made recommendations to revise the seven Rochdale Co-operative Principles in 1995 for the International Co-operative Alliance.

we share everything, but we don't control everything. A co-op is all about self-help—whatever we make, we share. Some people don't understand that.

If a co-op movement had existed in the North before the HBC trading posts were established, we wouldn't need a welfare system today. People would have been self-sufficient instead of having to depend on the HBC. What did Inuit get back from the HBC? The money spent by Inuit at those trading posts went to England, southern Canada, or the United States. But everything that a co-operative makes stays right there in the community. It's all about retaining wealth.

In Cambridge Bay, when we opened up our grocery store, eighty percent of the stuff we put on the shelves was cheaper than at the HBC store. Obviously, they had been making a substantial profit on us for years and years. I like to think that the Queen should hand us back our wealth and say, "Look you all, split this up between you!"[3] If we had had a co-op system in the North, poverty would not exist today. People would own their own houses, for example. Housing is expensive, but with determination and cooperation together, you can achieve a lot.

Outside of the government, the co-operatives are the biggest employers of aboriginal people in the North. The co-op system in the North is fifty years old. Especially in the earlier years, it was a professional training ground for a lot of people. James Arvaluk, John Ningark, Willie Adams, Louis Tapardjuk, Raymond Ningeocheak, Jack Anawak—they all started out at the co-op level and went on to hold good jobs within the government or within the Inuit organizations.

The co-op system also hires a lot of people that nobody else bothers to employ. We can train people in janitorial work, gas station work, workplace safety, and then they acquire meaningful skills with which they can earn a living.

---

3. The HBC was formerly a British Crown corporation.

Each community is sophisticated enough to know which people to hire and how to give them the proper training. Some of these people might have some kind of handicap or a lack of education, and while other employers might decide they're not suitable for work, we are glad to be able to train them for all kinds of things, even for menial jobs. We also hire local people who may not want to leave their hometown to move elsewhere for work.

The retention of good staff is crucial. A high employee turnover in the smaller communities is usually a sign that people are being hired from outside the community. Employee retention is higher when people are hired and trained within their own communities. That means when the government is initiating a project in a community, it should partner with local organizations. Take janitorial work, for instance: We shouldn't need to bring up workers from Toronto to clean government offices. That is the way it is being done right now, though! There are people in our communities who could do a lot of the jobs that are given to people from down South. When they come up here, you have to fly them into the settlements and find them housing. Those costs would be eliminated if northern employers hired and trained local people, even if it took a little longer to train them.

There is another problem that goes along with that. When I attended the co-operative management training program, there were thirty-seven of us in the class. Most of us are now working at better paying jobs for the government or in other organizations. The would-be managers in our communities all get snatched up by the government. Manager trainees or assistant managers often leave for that reason.

If you look at the HBC-owned Northern stores in the communities, you will likely see more non-Inuit people working with them than you would see at the co-op stores. In Cambridge Bay, the co-operative hires about twenty-seven employees, and only about three of them are non-Inuit

A Christmas sale at the Co-op.

Photo Credit: Arctic Co-operatives Limited

The Honourable John Munroe, Bill Lyall, Willie Adams, and S. Attagatok.

Photo credit: Arctic Co-operatives Limited

people working full time. In the store itself, we employ one non-Inuit person, our manager, who we hired thirteen years ago. When the board of directors talks to her about trying to hire somebody from elsewhere, she says, "No, no, no! We'll find somebody here! It will take longer but we will find somebody." I agree with her: No matter how much effort it takes, we have to try to hire and train local people.

Canadian Arctic Producers

The federal government used to own fifty percent of Canadian Arctic Producers. We, from Canadian Arctic Co-operatives Federation Limited (CACFL), negotiated with them so that it would finally belong to the people. In 1980, John Munroe, the Minister of the Department of Indian Affairs and Northern Development at the time, signed it over to CACFL.[4] The negotiations with the government were very hard, and once we gained control over CAP, our main challenge was to get back our strength and do it on our own.

The NWT Department of Economic Development and Tourism was responsible for the co-ops. Every year we made a motion to have the name changed to "Department of Economic Development, Tourism and Co-operatives", but they never accepted. They did have a supervisor of co-operatives. In those days, Canadian Arctic Producers was the marketing arm of the arctic co-operative movement, and they bought back everything that local co-ops would buy from their community artists. At CACFL, we felt that the territorial government wasn't marketing the products as well as they could. The NWT government people would

---

4. John Munroe was Minister of Indian Affairs and Northern Development in 1980, in the Liberal cabinet of Pierre E. Trudeau, when the Canadian Arctic Co-operative Federation Limited amalgamated with Canadian Arctic Producers. Prior to that, CAP had been a creation of the government with government-appointed directors on its board of administration. Louis Tapardjuk was then the president of CACFL. See: Mitchell 1996, 253-270.

come into our communities once a year with an arts and crafts trading budget to spend, and they would buy up a lot of carvings.[5] They had a whole basement full of them in Yellowknife. When those economic development people came to town, you would see seventy-five artists getting busy carving and making $300 a day, but as soon as these government people left town, there would only be the usual six carvers working again.

Nowadays there are a lot of other people who buy carvings, such as teachers, preachers, and RCMP officers. They are all busy buying Inuit art and selling it down south. There is also a big art auction sale every year in Toronto. But all these buyers are not very good channels for artists. The channels that we at the co-op developed are designed to build the careers of our artists. If you are a good artist and you make very good art, Canadian Arctic Producers will help you. We did that for a lot of people.

Today, in Iqaluit, many people are trying to sell carvings themselves. One morning when I was there, a carver was trying to sell a piece for $875 in the restaurant at breakfast time. At 11:30 that night, my brother bought it for $85. If that carver had been under the auspices of our organization, with our art dealers, we could have worked to build that person's reputation as a renowned artist. We have done that. We have sent artists away to carve in front of the Queen or at art shows, and they became recognized and appreciated. We also helped the Holman Island and Baker Lake print makers. Cape Dorset had its own marketing operation, run by Terry Ryan for many years.[6]

---

5. "Carvers" and "carvings" are Northern parlance for "sculptors" and "sculptures".
6. Terry Ryan became the general manager of the West Baffin Eskimo Co-operative after its founder James Houston left Cape Dorset in 1960. Under Ryan's management, the West Baffin Eskimo Co-operative decided to leave Canadian Arctic Producers and develop its own marketing organization, Dorset Fine Arts. Ryan was the executive director of Dorset Fine Arts in Toronto until his life partner

Some of the smaller co-operatives are reluctant to work with Arctic Co-operatives Limited because they don't want to pay a service fee to buy things through us. Really, it is because they don't understand the business advantages. The way we look at it, our service fee of seven per cent is very cheap. It lets us buy millions of dollars' worth of merchandise at big savings, which we can pass on to them. If they were to calculate what they would receive back from the Artic Co-operative Development Fund through Arctic Co-operatives Ltd, the service fee would be only four per cent.[7] Another bonus is that the share of the profits from the co-operatives gets higher every year because our revenues grow. But they don't understand that right now.

I don't believe that our arts and crafts operation was ever profitable, and I don't think there will be a demand for it in the future, either. We still buy art, but it is a service to the people, a way to help some of our members grow as artists. Back when the government was involved, they used to just buy without ever bothering to market the stuff and make a profit. We have a lot of inventory in Mississauga now, at our headquarters, but it is a lot of work, and very costly, to sell and ship.[8] When I first became chair of the co-operatives federation, sixty per cent of the agenda at our annual general meeting would be set aside to discuss carving issues. Today, it might not even be discussed at all.

Supporting arts and crafts in the North is really about helping people to help themselves. But if you buy a carving individually, from someone selling a piece from table to table in a restaurant, they sell it mostly to go out partying.

Leslie Boyd Ryan took over. Terry Ryan received the Order of Canada for his outstanding contribution to Inuit art.

7. The Arctic Co-operative Development Fund provides financial services to its member co-operatives in order to help them attain financial stability.

8. Canadian Arctic Producers' art showroom is at 2891 Slough St, Mississauga, ON L4T 1G4.

They probably don't use that money to feed their families. I bought a couple of pieces in Iqaluit, and I felt very guilty about it afterwards. I thought that instead of giving money to this person, who probably wasn't even the carver, I should have encouraged that man to sell his artwork to a dealer who could have promoted him properly. He should have gotten some recognition from the art world for his beautiful work. By buying it personally, I didn't really help that person.

Challenges for the co-op movement in the North

Like any other native organization, we try hard to get subsidies for training through government economic development programs. I believe we should be getting government assistance, especially because the co-op system has always been a training ground for many of the people recruited by the government. One year, half the Members of the Legislative Assembly sitting in Iqaluit were people who started their career in the co-op system.

We encounter a lot of resistance. It is a general attitude that we notice all the time, both from government and from non-Inuit business owners. After all, we employ close to one thousand aboriginal people. The social assistance money that the government gives to people stays in the North through the co-op system, but before the creation of the co-ops, that money would have circulated back down South. Even some of the people we employ in the settlements don't fully support their own co-ops. They travel to Yellowknife or Edmonton and come back with boxes loaded full of consumer goods.

It is sad that there is so much competition with us to provide services in the North. One area where that really comes up is in financial services. We do currently offer some banking services to our membership, but because we're not a bank, we are not insured if we lose money along the way. In 1996, Arctic Co-operatives Ltd proposed a credit union-type banking service for every community in Nunavut.

We had researched the idea of providing financial services through our co-op stores for communities of sixty-five people and more, such as Sachs Harbour, where other banks wouldn't want to go. Unlike us, the big banks go into a community to make money. Right from the beginning we went to the big banks to say we could partner with them to offer community services, and in every case they told us that they were not in the business of servicing people. They were in the business of making money.

In 1996, we were very close to securing the proper financial insurance. The federal and Northwest Territories governments, and co-operatives and credit unions across Canada were supporting the main part of the deal, and the credit unions had also offered to provide free training for five years. We asked Nunavut Tunngavik Inc. for a grant of $1 million, which we would match with our own $1 million. In fact, we raised close to $6 million. The board of directors at NTI didn't agree with our proposal.[9] The banking services plan is still on our agenda, however, and we are now working on it with the co-operatives and credit unions in Canada.[10] The co-operatives have to be involved in finance. It is not right that people in smaller communities have to go to Iqaluit to do their banking at those big institutions.

The same kind of resistance is happening with the arts and the government of Nunavut. The co-ops are the only major art dealers in Nunavut, but the government started an arts council without consulting us.[11] We asked to be

---

9. See: http://www.nunatsiaqonline.ca/archives/41029/news/nunavut/41029_07.html
10. See: http://www.cucentral.ca/.
11. The Nunavut Arts Council was established in 2001by the Government of Nunavut's Department of Culture, Language, Elders and Youth. See: http://www.gov.nu.ca/Files/policies/acp.pdf.

part of it, because we saw that the way it was organized wasn't in the best interests of the carvers.

The Housing Crisis in Nunavut

Partnering with the government is essential in the North. The main cause of high prices is the high cost of transportation. If the co-op movement could help more, we could get a lot of things done. With the Nunavut Housing Corporation, for instance, we could sit down with the government and have a productive chat about housing co-operatives.[12] In Yellowknife, we have two housing projects that function well: the Borealis Housing Co-op and the Inuksuk Housing Co-op.

A lot of Inuit in the communities live on welfare. They live in social housing, which is subsidized by the government, and so they have no incentive to work and be productive. In a housing co-op, you could get more local people involved at every level. The board of directors makes sure people pay their rent and take care of the property, and they could hire local people to do the maintenance of the buildings. People who co-own houses take more pride in the environment in which they live.

Another idea would be to have the co-operative movement run the Nunavut Housing Corporation. Right now, it is all operated by government personnel. I am not exactly sure how it could be done logistically, but I am sure there is a way. I believe that any government operated programs could be run in a co-operative way, so that the people are the owners. Elected politicians should be looking

12. The Nunavut Housing Corporation is a territorial government agency created in 2000. Its mandate is to provide access to affordable housing to the population of Nunavut. Of a total of 8,550 occupied dwellings in Nunavut in 2010, 4,400 are part of the subsidized social housing program. See: http://www.eia.gov.nu.ca/stats/Housing/Other%20 Documents/Analysis%20of%20the%20Housing%20Needs%20in%20 Nunavut,%202009-2010.pdf

at this kind of thing. A lot of government programs have not been successful, but if they would add in participation and ownership by the people, it would inspire people and make things work. We ought to be able to sit down and talk about how to invest in the people, so that when a project gets off the ground, their ownership counts.

When something is run by a co-op, the sense of ownership is there, and people take their responsibilities to heart. If a board of directors sees that things are not running right, it will figure out how to do it better. Ownership counts.

Chapter 6

Everything Revolves Around Money

I have worked for the co-op movement all my life and never thought much about savings. I always tried to put aside some money, but when you live in a small community in the North, it is hard to save substantial amounts. That is part of the reason why I started my fly fishing camp later on in life. I was reaching the age of sixty-five and thought it would be a way to survive in my retirement. I thought my fishing camp would be something I could do for a couple of months of the year, but it became real work and now it is part of my life. If you want to work at something, you have to make it worthwhile. So far I have been lucky, and since I started in 1999 I have had a full camp every summer. Hopefully it will continue like that until I leave.

The camp consists of eight buildings. I have a cook shack that can sit twenty-five to thirty people at a time, and I have five guest cabins as well as a cabin for myself and for the people working with me. It is very good fishing country up here, because we still have clean water. This part of the Arctic is really the last frontier, and we are working at bringing people up to see it. I tell my guests every year that it might be the last time they see something as pristine as this.

I make sure all my guests understand that we need to keep the environment clean. We do catch-and-release fly fishing. We only keep the fish that would die anyway, and we keep them to feed the guests. If we have to keep more than we can eat fresh that day, I make dry fish out of them. One of the other reasons we do catch-and-release is because we're fighting weather all the time, and we are using airplanes that can only carry a limited amount of weight. If people want to take fish home, they buy it in Cambridge Bay, where we have a commercial fishery plant. That way, guests can fly it out and not have to worry about losing it if the weather delays their flight out of the camp. Arctic char is a delicate fish and doesn't last very long if you don't have a proper way to keep it. The type of people who come to my catch-and-release camp don't mind the way we do it. They come to experience a fighting fish. A lot of those people travel all around the world to go fly fishing. It is just a hobby, and believe it or not, a lot of them don't even eat fish! They have the money to do that.

The Need for a Strong Social Economy

Many times during the years I was working for the co-op in Cambridge Bay or at the federation, people asked if I would go work for them. They promised me all kinds of money, but I always told them that I was with the co-op because I was trying to do something for my people. That is the essence of my life. It is a commitment that I made very early on, and I would do it all over again. I take any chance I see to help people do something better for themselves. If I had spent my adult life in the South, I would have most likely ended up advocating for people in the slums. I would have wanted to help other people do whatever was needed for them to get along better in their everyday lives. We are very new at this game, we Inuit people. I happened to be born in this part of the world in this day and age, and maybe when I'm gone my work will show.

In the early days in the North, the co-ops were little more than government make-work programs.[1] I'm not sure if the government could invest in the Cambridge Bay fishery now, the way they did in 1959. Then, it was economically viable to fish within one hundred miles of the fish plant in Cambridge Bay, but now I don't think it is viable even within a forty-mile radius. With the costs of airplanes and labour today, the Nunavut Development Corporation must take some losses. The fishery is practically a part of the social assistance system now, providing a place for people to work in town.

Social assistance is a big part of life in the North. The current policies do not really help people, because they act as disincentives to work and be productive. If you are on social assistance and social services finds out you have had some work, your rent goes up. Nowadays, the age group between twenty and forty knows how to manipulate that system. It is in the culture now. A lot of kids grow up thinking that social assistance is a valid way of life because they saw their parents living that way. A lot of young people don't want to leave the community to go find jobs in Toronto. A lot of them don't hunt, either. It is not part of their lifestyle anymore. In my own family, among my kids, there isn't a single hunter. Out of my own twelve siblings, only

---

1. In her book *From Talking Chiefs to a Native Corporate Elite*, Marybelle Mitchell uses the expression "the Little Colombo plan" to qualify the federal government's development strategy in the Arctic (Mitchell, 145-163). Donald Snowden, chief of the Industrial Division of the Department of Northern Affairs and National Resources, initiated a first co-operative project in George River, now Kangiqsualujjuaq, in 1958. For Snowden, the co-operative was the right institution to promote economic development in the Arctic (Iglauer, 23). The George River experiment was a success, and Snowden and his team launched a series of production co-operatives across the North. The federal government actively supported the development of production co-operatives, most specifically by creating Canadian Arctic Producers, a marketing agency for Inuit arts and crafts.

three of us were really hunters. The rest just go fishing once in a while.

There is a need to talk about the social economy in the North. Everything has to be tied in with it. It all comes down to poverty. A few years ago, the federal government was talking about eliminating poverty, but we know that without raising taxes, we will not be able to help the poor. Once in a while the New Democratic Party talks about poverty, but if they were ever to form a government, they wouldn't be able to do anything about it either, because Canadians would never permit them to raise taxes.

To me it seems as if the public housing policies and social assistance are just another kind of abuse towards the Inuit. What do you do when you have created a generation of people who are mostly dependent on social assistance? Many people are like that in the settlements. How do we go back and change that?

Everything revolves around money now. There is nothing you can do without it. If you run out of work or get hurt or get too old, you are out of luck! In Yellowknife, you see some aboriginal people walking down the street with a cane. What kind of work can they do? They end up going to social services. My father started to receive his old age pension cheques when he was sixty-five, and he didn't even want to cash them. He would say, "These cheques are for people who cannot do anything for themselves. They are for people who need it more than I do. I have a house. I'm living okay." We had to convince him to cash the cheques, telling him that if he didn't the government would just send replacements.

What if, right at the beginning, when the government first started drawing people into the settlements, they had told people, "Instead of giving you free housing, everybody will pay $400 a month." It might have taken a little longer for people to come out from the land, but they would have had to find a way to pay $400 a month to live in a nice house. People would have learned from the start that if you miss your rent, you owe twice that much the next month. If you don't pay, you are out the door. Maybe if it had been like that from the beginning, we would have a better housing situation today. At Arctic Co-operatives, we have co-op housing, but tenants are made to understand that it costs $580 a month for rent and they have to pay for fuel and electricity. It keeps the board of directors busy, but it works.

What will happen if, one day, the government has no more money to give out as social assistance? Will people starve? I don't see people coming out of this system of dependency. If you are regularly intoxicated, you are not going to come out of that overnight. You are dependent on the government and you won't all of a sudden be able to start paying for a house. It will be challenging to find a regular job if you have had a substance abuse problem for the last twenty-five years. In the North we have a very desperate situation. There is no other word for it.

At the co-op we sometimes give a person work because they are always begging for food. Our general manager buys them food. Most of the time we have to let them go because they can't change their habits and they keep making the same mistakes over and over. It is a big challenge for the co-operatives to keep our local people employed and to train them to be responsible enough to take on management positions. For an individual who is serious about moving ahead in their work, it more or less means cutting themselves off from their peers.

All we can do in the North right now is try to live by our seven principles of the co-operatives. They are all humane principles, and we know we are not failing as long as we keep trying. We only fail when we quit trying. In the long term, we need to convince the government that we need training money. We want to tell the Canadian government that the co-ops want to help them educate people about what real life is. Real life is not booze and drugs. Real life is an honest day's work for an honest day's pay. Let's teach our children that we all have struggles in life and that we still have to get up and put in an honest day's work. I have that fight with myself, as I get along in age. But even when I ache like hell in the morning, I just get up and do something to get going.

Chapter 7

Keeping Up With Progress

We have to get Inuit to understand that the co-operative system is there for them. If we put $140,000 a month out into the streets of Cambridge Bay in wages, we are helping the government. That is money that they don't have to throw into social services. But we need help from the government for that in the form of training dollars. We need to do staff training and board of directors training. It is hard to find the resources to keep that going. That kind of education is a must.

Now that we live in centralized communities we know what poverty is. People sink into poverty when they do not have jobs. We will never eliminate poverty, but we have to find a way to compensate for it with education and training. We need to find ways to partner with governments and companies and organizations, because we know best what is needed in the communities. Whenever a new entity comes into a community, we should be partnering with them. We should be in partnership with the mining companies. We can't stop progress, so if development happens we have to make sure that there is compensation. We have to make sure that at least fifty percent of the work force comes from the surrounding area.

At the same time, all the organizations are fighting for the same human resources from the available work force. About half of the labour pool will be people who can hold down good jobs. The other half are the ones fighting poverty, jumping from job to job or having addictions. We have to get all these people educated.

On Language

Arctic Co-operatives Limited goes along with the government's language policies.[1] We are the first ones to say that we want the Inuit language to stay alive. We try to stay aligned with the Nunavut Language Commission, so we use Inuinnaqtun signage. Unfortunately, it costs money to change all our signage, and we have to pass that cost down to the consumers, and that matters. In Cambridge Bay, our co-op staff speaks English. Nobody speaks Inuinnaqtun. A lot of our elders speak perfect English, but when they come to the store they speak to our young employees in Inuinnaqtun. The young people will say, "Bill, we need your help!" The Inuit language is becoming less spoken all over Nunavut.

I don't speak Inuktitut very fluently either.[2] When I went to residential school, I completely lost my own language. It is stuck in my brain somewhere, but it can't come out properly anymore. If I were to go to a camp where only Inuinnaqtun was spoken, I could get along, but in the world of commerce, I probably couldn't. When I first visited Tuktoyaktuk in 1950, not many people were still using their Inuit language. They had already been

1. The Inuit Language Protection Act was passed by the Legislative Assembly of Nunavut in September 2008. "It guarantees the right to Inuit language education, defining specific obligations for public services, private businesses and protecting unilingual and bilingual employees of the territorial government who choose to work in Inuktitut." Source: http://www.nunatsiaqonline.ca/stories/article/65674nunavut_language_laws_a_priority_aariak_says/.
2. Bill Lyall's maternal relatives originally came from Cape Dorset. In his early childhood, Bill Lyall was exposed to a South Baffin dialect. In the Cambridge Bay area, Inuinnaqtun is the prevailing dialect. The latter is recognized as an official language by the Government of Nunavut, even though it has been largely abandoned by younger generations of Inuit.

influenced by non-Inuit coming from the West, from the Mackenzie Delta, and from the whalers' descendents. The schools are now teaching Inuktitut, but if kids don't use it at home, they won't keep it up. East of Cambridge Bay, though, it is more common to hear kids speaking Inuktitut.

I think the French language is going in the same direction across Canada. I used to hear much more French when I travelled to Winnipeg, and even in Quebec City, now, people switch to English when I ask, "How much?" English is winning out over French, as it is with Inuktitut. My late father used to say that in twenty-five or thirty years we wouldn't hear Inuktitut anymore, and I think he was right.

New Media

New technology has changed Northern people. When television first came to the communities, I resisted it because I had seen the changes it was causing everywhere else. Every night, even when my kids had to go to school the next morning, I had to go and round them up from all the places around the community where they were watching TV. That is why I eventually bought a TV set. I have pictures at home of five, six, or seven kids all sitting in my living room watching TV. You can't rebel against such things for very long!

When computers came in, I resisted them too. Now I see my kids typing away on their computers all day long. I am still resisting that—I will not buy a computer for myself. Sometimes people at work tell me I should get a laptop, but I tell them I let the secretary do the laptop work. I write a few things down on paper and ask her to fill it in with words. Then she sends it out on the Internet. I have used a laptop before, but I prefer to use a fax machine if I have to send out a communication of some sort. I have no problem with e-commerce. It is an important business tool, and it is an important part of our marketing.

One friend told me recently that he'd spent two hours on his computer on a Monday morning catching up on e-mails. I said, "You wasted two hours doing that? You should have been outside, rolling barrels of fuel or something!" People at work waste time sending messages to each other all day. It was happening in our office, on co-op time. If you walk around some offices, you often see people playing solitaire on their computers.

I have had to be involved in the decision to fire someone for using their computer at work to do things that were not very good. Although we have very strict rules about the use of our computers and the Internet, we have seen several teenaged part-time employees misuse it. They use Facebook to discredit or belittle each other. In a small community like Cambridge Bay, that can be destructive.

Still, I can see that technology is a good thing. Progress is not something that we will ever be able to stop, so we need to keep up with it as much as we can. Arctic Co-operatives Ltd members own the cable system in twenty-five Nunavut communities, and we provide the cable service in Iqaluit. It is a very efficient way of communicating. We are working with Isuma TV to diffuse their very good Inuit cultural programming; eventually we would like it to reach all the communities in the North.[3] Nowadays, there is not much Inuktitut programming on APTN.[4] It is mostly First Nations programming.

---

3. Arctic Co-operatives Limited is partnering with Isuma TV to make that company's productions available to communities via the local cable system. The service is presently available in Igloolik, Pangnirtung, Iqaluit, Rankin Inlet, and Pond Inlet.

4. Television Northern Canada (TVNC) was created in 1991. It broadcast only to the Northwest Territories and Yukon until it became a national broadcaster in 1999, at which point it became the Aboriginal Peoples Television Network, based in Winnipeg. [Since the creation of APTN, many Inuit have been heard to object to the reduction in Inuktitut programming-hours that were a result of the change. Another common complaint is that the broadcaster appears to be more oriented towards English-speaking aboriginals. —editor]

Apparently the Inuit Broadcasting Corporation is sending material there to be broadcast, but it isn't aired.[5] Inuit have been lumped in with the aboriginal population, but we need and want specifically Inuit programming. The media space should be shared properly.

Arctic Co-operatives Ltd could be providing broadband Internet to northern communities with our cable system, but another company in the Kitikmeot region manages the signal.[6] I think we could provide that service in a better way, but we don't want to compete with them because they are funded by a land claims organization. If we could use our cable system, we would have much more speed.[7] We do partner with Northwestel, Nunasi Development Corporation, and with aboriginal groups in Ardicom.[8]

Partnering

Navigating partnerships can be complicated for Arctic Co-operatives Ltd. We try to work with the land claims

---

5. The Inuit Broadcasting Corporation is a publicly funded Inuit media production corporation. IBC is an offspring of the Inuksuk Project created in the 1970s to produce and broadcast Inuktitut programming through the satellite Anik B. Inuit were then exploring an alternative to southern television channels.

6. The broadband Internet signal managed by PolarNet is a division of the Kitikmeot Corporation, an Inuit regional land claims organization.

7. Only twenty-seven percent of the Nunavut population has access to high speed Internet. The average Internet speed in Nunavut is five times slower than that of southern Canada. As of publishing, there is no cable Internet access available in the territory. See: http://www.nunatsiaqonline.ca/stories/article/65674nunavuts_internet_lags_behind_the_rest_of_canada_crtc/

8. Nunasi Corporation is the business arm of Nunavut Tunngavik Inc., the Inuit organization responsible for the implementation of the Nunavut Land Claims Agreement. Northwestel is a telephone company servicing Yukon, Northwest Territories, and Nunavut. Ardicom is a partnership between Arctic Co-operatives Ltd, Northwestel, and NASCo (Northern Aboriginal Services Company); it provides a digital communication network for local Internet service providers.

organizations, but sometimes they partner with companies in direct competition with us. For instance, we had to start our own shipping company when two Inuit beneficiaries' corporations joined forces with the HBC to start Nunavut Eastern Arctic Shipping (NEAS).[9,10] As soon as we saw that we thought, "You know what? We will be asking our competitor to carry our freight in a few years if we don't do something." Now, we are the seventy-five-percent owners of Nunavut Sealink and Supply Inc., with Transport Desgagnés.[11] That partnership benefits all the communities and all the partners in the company. We made that move because obviously we do not want to rely on the HBC, our competitors, to move our freight.

Transport Desgagnés has been a family company for over ninety years. They use their ships twelve months of the year, which keeps their overhead down. NTCL runs only for four months of the year, while the water is open, and the rest of the time their ships are sitting at the dock. Northerners pay for that through freight costs. With NSSI we have done more in-kind work for the government of Nunavut than NTCL ever did in all the time that they were in operation. In the past years, we shipped one house to each community for the Nunavut Housing Corporation as a corporate gift.

---

9. Nunasi Corporation and the Inuvialuit Regional Corporation.
10. Headquartered in Iqaluit, NEAS is majority-owned by local Inuit birthright corporations. Initially, shareholders included Qikiqtaaluk Corporation and Sakku Investment Corporation from Nunavut and Makivik Corporation from Nunavik. This group of controlling shareholders is joined by Transport Nanuk, a Canadian maritime carrier which has operated in the North for more than half a century. See: http://www.neas.ca/commitment.cfm. As of September 2011, Sakku and Qikiqtaluk corporations sold their shares in NEAS to Makivik and bought shares in NSSI instead. See http://www.nunatsiaqonline.ca/stories/article/65674qikiqtaaluk_sakku_investments_buy_into_nssi/.
11. Transport Desgagnés, based in Quebec, has been a leader in Eastern Arctic maritime shipping since the 1980s.

We now have the NNI certification with Transport Desgagnés and we tender successfully when the Government of Nunavut is giving out shipping contracts. We deliver dry cargo to all Nunavut communities except for Iqaluit.[12] The year that we got the government contract to do their shipping, Transport Desgagnés built another ship right away and had it in the water the following year. That ship cost $40 million! They are very flexible that way. The first year, we sailed the ship all the way to Kugluktuk and back to St. Catharines, Ontario, in 58 days. Two days later it had a fresh crew and was heading to Saudi Arabia on a contract.

We still buy most of our products from Western Canada. It is cheaper to buy goods there and truck them to St. Catharines for shipping than it is to truck them up to the ship in Hay River. As soon as you go North, your freight costs go sky high because of the price of fuel. In the future, we will probably begin to buy more in the East to save on trucking costs, but as long as we are shipping from Hay River, we will still buy from the West. We service some fifty-odd communities over an area that is one-third of the landmass of Canada. That is very costly.

Sustainability

It takes a lot to succeed in a sustainable business, because when you produce locally, the costs are too high. Even the local fisheries cost too much because of the transportation and processing costs. In Iqaluit, we are putting together some great assets, with four or five new ventures, but we have to run things as a corporate business

---

12. NNI: Nunavummi Nangminiqaqtunik Ikajuuti Registry. Inuit businesses from Nunavut can register with the NNI to have better chances to win business contracts from the Nunavut government. It is a GN strategy to support Nunavut Inuit-owned businesses that are in compliance with the Nunavut Land Claims agreement (NLCA).

because there is no local board.[13] It would be much better if local people got involved, because then they would receive the benefits. Right now those benefits are split between all the co-ops. Unfortunately, not many Iqaluit businesses are owned by local Inuit.

We once started a bakery in Cambridge Bay, back when Andrew Goussaert was still working there. We bought an oven that used three-phase power, which lets you make 100 loaves at a time. But to pay for that electricity, we had to make 500 loaves a day. That was too much for Cambridge Bay. We tried to sell to other communities, but the high transportation costs made a loaf of our bread cost something like $8 in Kugaaruk. We had to shut it down.

It is not even worthwhile to make your own clothes anymore. Today, you pay $40 per metre for the duffle, where we used to only pay $8. The outer layer, "Canadian mist", costs $40 per metre, where it used to be $4 or $5 per metre.[14] Then you have to buy the fur from a company in Alberta. If you want good fur, you buy wolverine, which costs $1,200 for a skin from Russia. It used to cost under $100 to make a parka, and now it would cost more than ten times that. It is better to buy a $500 Woods parka from the store than to make your own! The only homemade things I have are my footwear. I have mukluks with a duffle for when I travel. Regular boots are warm enough for being on the snowmobile.

I try to stick to eating country food because the doctors tell you that anything you shoot or you catch yourself off the land is good food. There are quite a few people doing that. If you buy pork or beef, you are eating all the enhancements they put in the animals to make them grow or to prevent

---

13. Arctic Co-operatives Ltd directly owns the co-operative ventures in Iqaluit. To this day, Iqaluit residents have never been able to set up a strong local co-operative organization.

14. Canadian mist is a water resistant fabric made out of cotton and nylon. It is an excellent material for parkas.

illness. It is much better to eat what you shoot off the land. I got twelve caribou in October, and what we don't eat over the winter, I will thaw out in June and use to make dried meat for the next winter. Most people don't do that kind of stuff anymore.

You need nice weather to make dry fish. With a good warm wind, you can dry fish in a week and put it away for the winter. If you don't want seagulls to get at your meat, you have to use one as a scarecrow: you shoot one down and hang it up by your food. Other seagulls won't come then. Unless you are in a settlement, ravens won't bother much with that kind of thing.

Looking Forward

It is hard to know what will happen to the co-op movement in the future. I don't see a lot of people trying to take it on and continue what we are doing. I wish there were more people who were interested in making sure that local people have a say and a share in what happens within their communities. People get busy in their everyday lives and aren't willing to be leaders. Even a lot of people who work for the co-operatives are only thinking about the next task at hand, rather than coming to sit in the boardroom and make decisions. People seem to think the way things run is not any of their business and they wait for others to do something. We need to get more people interested in taking on the driving and the decision making. There actually are some kids who are interested in the co-op. They work there after school. I try to convince young adults to run for our co-op's board of directors. Most of them don't make it as far as the boardroom, though, because they get better jobs.

When I was asked at the beginning if I would run for president of Arctic Producers, I said "yes" and then asked what I would have to do. The more I looked into it, the more I found it interesting, and the more I was willing to give it a try. I do that for everything. If somebody asks me to do something that I haven't done before, I'm usually willing. That's why I agreed to tell my story for a book. It is something I never really expected I would do, even though many people have asked me to write my life story. I always answered that there was nothing interesting for me to write about. I lived my everyday life, I just tried to raise a family and feed my children and my wife. But once I sat down and started talking about my life, I thought, "I did all that?"

Everything I've done has been to help people have a better life. When I look at today's young people, I think that they need to get an education if they're going to be part of the society we live in. The thing I really hope to see shaping up in the North is education. Our children have to understand that progress is not going to stop for them. We have to be part of progress to keep things on an even keel, for the territory and for ourselves. Getting an education is an absolute must for that.

Chapter 8

Owning Our Community Business

From an interview with Guy Enoapik,
member of the Whale Cove hamlet council
and long-time co-op supporter

I joined the Coral Harbour co-op as a member in 1972, when the Canadian Arctic Co-operative Federation (CACF) was formed in the Northwest Territories. The first annual general meeting of the federation took place in Churchill, Manitoba, that same year. Walter Porter was there; he has been involved since then. Andrew Goussaert was also a participant. There were delegates from all over the Arctic, even from Northern Quebec and Port Burwell. Port Burwell was a community that belonged to the Northwest Territories before the people were relocated to Nunavik.[1] The first office of the CACF was located in Yellowknife until 1986.

Before 1972, the co-operatives were run by their local communities, and they purchased their merchandise from private suppliers. There was no one organization to take care of us and provide what we needed. Even if the

---

1. Port Burwell was a community located on the island of Killinik, at the mouth of the Hudson Strait. The island is now part of Nunavut. The HBC opened a trading post there in 1885, Moravian missionaries established a mission in 1905, and the RCMP opened a station in 1920. All the inhabitants were moved to Nunavik in 1978. A co-op retail store was opened there in 1960, when the population of the island numbered only 23 individuals.

local co-op was managed by the community itself, people would still sometimes buy sugar from the Northern store because it was the fastest way to get it. In Whale Cove, where I live, they would run out of goods in those days, because there was little transportation in and out. In the springtime, when the ice was melting, no planes could fly in at all because there was no runway. Only float planes could come in and land when the lakes were fully thawed.

When the mine shut down in Rankin Inlet in 1962, some families moved to Whale Cove, and there were also several families from Arviat who lived there until the cannery closed.[2] At one time there were around four hundred people living in Whale Cove. People worked at whaling, sealing, and fishing. In those days people had a hard life, but there was a real knowledge of how to survive. There was only one area administrator at the time, and no interpreters.

In the early 1960s, the government opened a co-operative country food cannery. It ran for four or five years. Because it was the only employer in town, when it closed, the people from Arviat moved back to their own settlement. The population of Whale Cove dropped over the years, and in 1985, when I moved there, it had gone down to 203 inhabitants. When several more families moved away, it dropped to half that again. I pushed the government to do something to create employment in Whale Cove because I wanted to stay there, and my boys enjoyed living close to their grandparents. Economic development in the community has gone pretty well so far, and now the population is back up to around four hundred.

I joined the hamlet council in 1987. I made a motion to replace all the short telephone poles in the community, and

2. In 1965, a co-operative cannery was established in Whale Cove, under the direction of the Northern Affairs and National Resources Industrial Division team. The director Don Snowden undertook the ambitious task of marketing canned country food all across the Arctic. The project was abandoned after a few years.

after seven years, the government responded and replaced them with long ones. We also have a new power plant and five storage tanks for fuel and gas. When I moved there, there was only one fuel tank, and sometimes we almost ran out of gas. Right now, almost half the population in Whale Cove owns their home. The home owners program was cut off in 2004, though, and now people can only get what they call "access houses".

The co-op was really small when I arrived in Whale Cove. They worked amazingly hard to start it. The HBC had tried to open a trading post over in the Tavani area but had to close it down because of problems getting their ship around the reefs.[3] When they realized that Tavani was too shallow and dangerous, the people asked if they could have a co-op in Whale Cove. We are in deep water here, and we have two boat landings, one of them for big ships. They started a co-operative general store that sold groceries. The purchasing was then being taken care of by the Canadian Arctic Co-operative Federation Limited (CACFL), which shipped in food supplies, snow machines, and that kind of thing. The co-op also bought carvings in Whale Cove, when there was an interest from people down South to buy Inuit art. They still buy some from the carvers, but not as much these days. They also used to buy fox furs, although with the drop in the fur industry because of Greenpeace's activities, there is no more demand for those skins.

The late Walter Porter was leading the annual general meeting in 1972 down in Churchill, Manitoba, which was the incorporation meeting for the Canadian Arctic Co-operative Federation Limited (CACFL). His brother Ralph Porter was our leader. Ralph really wanted to help people to run their own businesses in their own communities. At that time, I was still living in Coral

---

3. Tavani, or Tavane, is located 31 kilometres south of Whale Cove. The HBC operated a trading post there in the early 1930s. *See: Niurrutiqarniq, Trading With the Hudson's Bay Company, Edited by Shannon Partridge. 2009. Nunavut Arctic College.*

Harbour and was involved in the co-op there. I went to that meeting in Churchill and brought a cheque of $100 for the membership of the Coral Harbour co-operative. At first I didn't work for the co-ops; I just gave out information. I wasn't even on the board because I had seen that I could do more by staying outside of the organization. I wanted to help make it more efficient and sustainable.

In Whale Cove, the co-op store is the only business. At one time some people there wanted to have a Northern store come into the community. That would have made it more difficult for our co-operative. I have been explaining for years what the co-op system is all about. The store is co-owned by the members, and for three straight years we have received dividends.

My goal in being involved in the co-op movement is to help the members survive and help the body of operations survive. We are not like a Northern store; the co-op is run by its own community. We are involved in the co-op movement, and Arctic Co-operatives Ltd is our federation. We are responsible for making it run. Some people think they can get free groceries when they become members of our co-op, and sometimes they forget to pay their outstanding balances. I want to support the individuals, but on the other hand, there has to be accountability to the whole co-op.

Whale Cove doesn't have things easy. The population is very small, and there are not many jobs. Only a small number of people have full-time jobs. If we had more resource people to run programs and help us figure out how to get things going, that would help us create more employment. We don't have a Nunavut Arctic College Learning Centre in Whale Cove anymore. I have been trying to get one, but there is a lack of interest in Arctic College programs here. In our case, we can't blame the government for not providing a service; part of our problem is just that people didn't demonstrate enough interest in getting educated. That is too bad, because getting an education is pretty well the only way to make things better.

I am the foreman for the hamlet of Whale Cove, and I have to look for qualified air brake drivers to run the sewage and water trucks and the loader and grader. Sometimes it is hard to find people who want to work. We have to find out how we can get more people interested, both in the short term for work and in the long term for future employment opportunities. We have to find incentives. If you are just standing up here waiting for a welfare cheque, that is no good in the long term.

We are very lucky in Whale Cove because there are a few good people who have been employed at our co-op for quite a number of years. They are very interested in their work. We have a good manager, a good assistant manager, and we also have a good office worker. We hire students to work after school or, if we have to, we hire them full time. We try to get young people working.

Often, the educated or talented people are just plucked out of the co-op system to go work in government offices. They go because they are able to get more benefits with government jobs. That is a really a big problem in co-operatives. The people working in a co-op office are handling a lot of responsibility and are well trained. They are taking care of money and ordering and managing people. That is why they are valuable to the government.

Chapter 9

We Don't Want to Be Controlled
by Somebody Else

*From an interview with Lucassie Arragutainaq,
President of the Mitiq Co-operative in Sanikiluaq,
Nunavut*

I was born at the south end of the Belcher Islands, which is where my parents were from. We have family in Quebec and Nunavut, and from Salluit all the way down to James Bay. My wife's father moved from Salluit to the Belcher Islands back in 1930s. We're all the same people, really.

When I was away from the community to go to school in the mid-1960s, I heard that a carving production co-operative was being created at home. In that original co-op, one branch grew up in the North Camp, one started in the South Camp, and they shared a board of directors made up of members from both sides.[1] The board of directors would first meet at the North Camp co-op and then travel to the South Camp co-op, using the same agenda with the people down there. The North and South Camps were some sixty miles apart.

---

1. Prior to 1970, there were two communities on Flaherty Island in the Belcher Islands: North Camp and South Camp. In 1970 the two communities merged at the location of the North Camp, forming the community of Sanikiluaq, where approximately 800 people live today. As the Belcher Islands are in the Hudson Bay, they fall under federal jurisdiction and are therefore part of Nunavut.

I am not sure exactly who came in and actually got things going, but I remember people were told they would have to pay $10 for their membership and at the end of the year they would get their money back. Expectations were high. I became a member in the early 1970s, after I came back from school and understood a little bit of English. I was first elected to the board of directors around 1973, which is when I started to know that I really wanted to help people. I kept getting re-elected and eventually became the chair of the board in 1979.

Lukassie Ikussukti was the chairman of the board when the co-op started. He looked after the $10,000 in funding that the co-op had received from the Department of Indian Affairs to start operations. When a group of government inspectors came to our community after a few years and asked about the $10,000, they asked to see Lukassie's records. Because he didn't understand that word in English, Lukassie went home to get his long-playing records! The government guy got confused and said, "No, I want to know how you spent that $10,000!" That was at the beginning, when we weren't used to working in English. There were records, though. Everything was written down on paper, such as how much money was spent and how many carvings were bought in a day. The bookkeeper who kept track of that is now an elder in the community.

The co-op was buying carvings, and the Hudson's Bay Company at the North Camp was buying carvings too. In summer, people used to go shopping at the HBC by boat. Because it would take up to six or seven hours to get there, depending on the weather, they started the small co-op at the South Camp. It was just a small shack where they sold all the basic stuff, such as flour, lard, tea, cigarettes, and sugar. They also bought carvings. These weren't cash exchanges; the clerk would write down how much the carvings cost and put the amount towards credit.

Back in those early days, some people felt caught between the HBC and the co-op. The HBC people at North

Camp had helped people a lot over the years, with things like medical care and radio communications. Some people felt bad about not supporting the HBC anymore, but they began to realize that with a private company, they had no say at all. People began to want to make a difference in their lives by supporting the co-op. I kept telling them that if they helped the co-op, it could help them. If people support the co-operative, they are not being controlled by somebody else—they are in control of themselves.

We didn't know much about the other co-ops back then, or about Canadian Arctic Co-operative Federation Limited (CACFL). In the early 1970s, we had heard that the Pelly Bay co-operative had bought a DC-4, but we really didn't have contact with any other co-ops.[2] In 1981 we learned that there was going to be an annual general meeting in Frobisher Bay (now Iqaluit), where the headquarters were, and we were interested in attending. Andrew Goussaert was the chief executive officer then.[3] We had heard about the CACFL meeting from Louis Tapardjuk, who was the chairperson of that organization at the time. We had had contact with Louis because he used to order movies for his co-op from the same company in Montreal that we ordered from.[4]

2. The community of Pelly Bay, now Kugaaruk, was beleaguered by sea-ice problems in the summer, when supply ships would normally bring goods. To solve the problem, the co-operative bought a DC-4 airplane. They later sold it to the CACFL when Andrew Goussaert, the former Oblate missionary at Pelly Bay, was the president of the federation. See foonote 3.
3. Before becoming chief executive officer of the Canadian Arctic Co-operative Federation Limited, Andrew Goussaert was a Roman Catholic missionary with the Order of the Oblates of Mary Immaculate. He devoted most of his life to the development of the co-operative movement in the Arctic. He now resides in Winnipeg, Manitoba with his family.
4. Louis Tapardjuk was the President of the Canadian Arctic Co-operatives Federation Limited from 1976 to 1981. He was a Member of the Nunavut Legislative Assembly from 2004 to 2013, representing the constituency of Amittuq.

The first time I met Bill Lyall was at that annual general meeting. I remember that when it was my turn to speak at the meeting, I talked for about six or seven minutes in Inuktitut. I spoke just as I do when I'm at home in Sanikiluaq. When I finished, the translator and everybody else just stared at me blankly. They hadn't understood a word of what I said! They said, "You guys talk very, very fast!" Nevertheless, that year an election was held for the board of directors of CACFL, and I got elected to it.

Bill Lyall is very direct and very supportive. He tells the members how things are and why they are like that. He doesn't give long speeches when it comes to issues, because that is the Inuit style of talking. I talk that way, too. There is a difference between *Qallunaat* and Inuit: I would say that a Qallunaaq will tell you all about how he caught a fish, but an Inuk doesn't care how you caught the fish, as long as you caught it. What we learned from Bill was to be truthful and direct.

Bill takes things very seriously at the board meetings, and then he becomes an ordinary person again after the meeting is over. It is good to do it that way. He is a friend of mine, and when we worked together at the board level, that didn't change our friendship. He tries to make things very simple for people to understand. Because of what I learned from him, I try to make my presentations of annual financial statements simple enough for our members to understand. People are not used to that kind of information. There are a lot of special terms used in the statements, words that don't yet have equivalents in Inuktitut, so we have to explain what they mean. I think the learning worked both ways in that respect—I learned from Bill, and he learned from me.

In Sanikiluaq today, our co-op is always trying to get the new generation coming up involved as members. We tell them, "Your grandfather was on the first board of directors. His membership number was sixty-five, and now your number will be in the three-thousands!"

Photo Credit: Arctic Co-operatives Limited

Photo Credit: Arctic Co-operatives Limited

Chapter 10

The Emergence of the
Arctic Co-operative Movement

From an interview with Andy Morrison,
Chief Executive Officer of Arctic Co-operatives Limited

> *"For any kind of co-op development, you've
> got to have the right combination of people."*

I got to know Bill Lyall when he became the first
President of Arctic Co-operatives Limited (Arctic
Co-operatives Ltd), in 1981, and I went on to work with
him for 28 years. Bill had first become involved in his local
co-operative, the Ikaluktutiaq Co-op of Cambridge Bay, in
the early 1970s, and then became its president a few years
later. In 1979 he was elected to the board of directors of
Canadian Arctic Producers Co-operative Limited (CAPCL
or CAP), and later, when Arctic Co-operatives Limited
became the management arm for CAPCL and the Canadian
Arctic Co-operative Federation Limited (CACFL), Bill
became the president of that new organization.

I started working with CACFL in 1981 just after the
annual general meeting that authorized the incorporation
of Arctic Co-operatives Ltd. In my early role I didn't
have direct contact with the board of directors. CACFL
became a hub for member co-operatives to access a variety

of services: purchasing and merchandizing, accounting, auditing, human resources, training, and education.

Initially CAP was not a co-operative. It was first incorporated in 1965 as a limited company and was restructured into a co-operative in 1979.[1] From then on, the co-operative movement in the Arctic had two federations: the CACFL and the CAP. When CAP became a co-operative, the members felt there was no longer a need for two federations, and the process began to amalgamate those two organizations. Because CAP was federally incorporated, and CACFL was only incorporated in the Northwest Territories, it took a while to amalgamate both entities. In 1981, a third co-operative was incorporated and called Arctic Co-operative Limited; it became the management co-operative for CAP and CACFL. In November 1982, those three organizations amalgamated in the organization that we have today, Arctic Co-operatives Ltd.

Co-operatives in the North developed as communities were settled and developed. Port Burwell's Kikitoayak Eskimo Co-operative and Cape Dorset's West Baffin Eskimo Co-operative were the first to be created in what was then the Northwest Territories.[2] In those days, people were still very much living a traditional lifestyle, hunting and fishing. As people moved into the communities,

1. Canadian Arctic Producers, created in 1965, was first a limited company supported by the Canadian Union of Co-operatives and was supported financially by the Department of Northern Affairs and National Resources. Alma Houston, the wife of John Houston, founding manager of the West Baffin Eskimo Co-operative, has been a driving force behind the CAP's development as a marketing agency for Inuit art.
2. Port Burwell was located on the island of Killiniq at the mouth of Hudson Strait. The Kikitoayak Eskimo Co-operative was established there in 1959. All inhabitants were relocated to Nunavik in 1978. Killiniq Island was part of the Northwest Territories until 1999, and is now part of Nunavut. The West Baffin Eskimo Co-operative was created with the diligent support of James Houston, a legendary figure within the Inuit art industry.

they did exactly what they did when they were living on the land: they provided for themselves and they shared. Trapping was a big part of the way of life, and people would sell the furs to the Hudson's Bay Company or to independent traders. People were not satisfied with the way they were treated. Some trappers and hunters started to sell their furs as a group, but not to the HBC. Instead, they started to sell directly to auctions in the South. Thirty years ago there were many auction houses in Canada, such as those in Thunder Bay, Vancouver, and Montreal.

Around that time, in the 1950s and '60s, Inuit art was becoming a commodity that had value in southern Canada. The art being produced then was much different than that of today. Many Inuit started making their own arrangements to send their art to the South, supported by the Co-operative Union of Canada.[3] Boxes and boxes of art from the Arctic were warehoused in their offices to be sold to dealers.

Eventually, the profits from these direct sales of furs and art would make their way back to the communities. It must have taken months and months for that money to make it back, perhaps even as long as a year. Some of the money that came back would go directly to the hunters and trappers and their families, and some of it would be used to build things in the communities. People would need to buy provisions, which eventually led to the beginning of co-operative retail stores. Flour, sugar, tea, and lard would be shipped in and people in the communities would buy them.

When the American military abandoned some of the DEW Line sites, people in the communities would recoup the buildings. They could haul a building across the tundra or dismantle a building nail by nail and re-assemble it in

---

3. The Co-operative Union of Canada was founded in 1909 and merged with the Co-operative College of Canada in 1987. That new entity, called the Canadian Co-operative Association, still exists today. See: http://www.coopscanada.coop.

the community. These were used as warehouses or retail stores or transient centres which, later, were developed into co-op hotels. People would also scavenge any equipment left behind at the DEW Line sites and put two or three pieces together to get a functional one. They could put together a grader or a loader for their community that way! People were very resourceful.

We Rely on Ourselves

Early on, there were a number of people who were equipped to offer advice and support for co-op development in the Arctic. From the government there were James Houston, Don Snowden, and Paul Godt, of the Department of Northern and Indian Affairs' industrial division.[4] There were also missionaries, such as Andrew Goussaert, who were living with Inuit and discussing with them how they could have more control over their lives and their economy.

The missionaries played a big role in developing arctic co-ops in many communities.[5] While some co-operatives evolved organically because of the art and fur trading that were taking place, others developed from commercial operations that had been organized by these missionaries. It would be interesting to examine the correlation between the development of the co-operatives and the development of the communities and see how things evolved differently in places where they didn't have such individuals. It would

---

4. In 1958, the Department of Northern Affairs and Natural Resources launched a five-year program, the Northern Co-operative Development Program (Mitchell, pp. 149-151).
5. Many Roman Catholic missionaries from the Missionary Oblates of Mary Immaculate played a pivotal role in developing Arctic co-operatives. Some notable figures were Andrew Goussaert (Pelly Bay and Cambridge Bay), Hans Van de Velde (Pelly Bay), Louis Fournier (Igloolik), Henry Tardy (Holman), and André Steinman (Puvirnituq) (Mitchell, 172).

show that in any kind of co-op development, you've got to have the right combination of people. Once the concept of an organized co-op would be presented to a community, its people would start wondering about all the possibilities. It is truly amazing how the development took place from that initial point. In those days, there were no co-op employees; people just supported each other and worked together. If a plane landed with supplies, they got together and handled the freight themselves. If you look at the Inuit and Dene cultures, you see that their way of life was always like that. The idea of co-ops fitted very well with the traditional way of life, which is all about working together and supporting each other.

As individuals began to see the impact the co-operatives had on their daily lives, they decided to push further, taking things to the next level of organization. They were willing to undergo a lot of hardship and do a lot of hard work to build their co-operatives. One example of that is in Igloolik, where there is, today, a monument to the memory of the late Pacôme Qulaut. He was a co-op leader who lost his life working to build something for the people there. His bulldozer went through the ice when he was bringing some scavenged equipment from an abandoned DEW Line site back to Igloolik. He showed others what they can do when they put their minds to it. It was all about starting small and growing, building something bigger one step at a time.

Conditions in the North were just right for things to start happening. Air service was starting, schools were being set up, and municipal administrations were being established. Many of the early co-operatives formalized and organized their operations. The model of a democratically owned and democratically controlled business entity made sense to people, and these organizations became what they are today. There were other changes that played a role as well. There had been a number of cases of starvation, and the migration of caribou had changed in some areas. Canada was severely criticized at the United Nations because of our treatment of aboriginal peoples in the Arctic. The government was starting to take more of an interest in the Arctic because of sovereignty issues and the Cold War. These factors were changing the government's attitude about providing support to people living in the Arctic.

Between 1965 and 1979, because the co-operatives sold Inuit art to CAP, their investment in CAP grew. The co-operatives of the Arctic were shareholders in CAP, but they didn't have any economic control over the organization. When the co-operatives gained greater economic control over the company's administration, they wanted to convert it into a co-operative. Initially there was absolute financial support from the government of Canada in developing CAP. That was the first time where local co-operatives worked together in one economic entity.

As people gained economic strength at the community level, they began to wonder what opportunities would be created by a couple of community co-ops working together at a regional level or right across the North. Discussions ensued about forming a second-tier co-operative or a federation of co-operatives. One of the main hurdles to overcome was the huge geographic area the NWT encompassed. At the time, the NWT covered one third of the land mass of Canada and included some fifty-eight communities. But these were new settlements that had just sprung up in the 1950s and '60s, and most of them didn't have roads or regular air service.

To try to get people together to talk about an idea was a huge challenge. If you look at Nunavik, which is very small, you see that they were able to come together much quicker. They had an existing political structure in the South and a provincial government that could support their co-operatives, whereas in the NWT, there were no local government structures before 1967. Despite the obstacles, or perhaps because of their nature, the notion of forming a federation of co-operatives developed very early on.

The logistics of running these co-ops individually were amazingly complicated. If they wanted to send out furs, there was often no regular air service to do so. There were no banks, there was no mail service, and there were no telephones. When a co-op finally got some money back from furs or art sent south, there were no retail businesses in their home communities where they could buy provisions. And once they had created a business, the co-ops had to report to the government, do financial statements, pay income tax, and deduct income tax when they had employees. Individually, they couldn't afford to hire accountants. They saw that it would be possible, however, if they grouped together to hire an accountant. It would be possible to get discounts on goods by making purchases together. Quebec co-ops grouped together in a federation in 1967, and in the NWT they did it in 1972.

On Bill Lyall

Bill has taken a lot of jibes from people over his commitment and his dedication to the co-operatives. Many people have become very wealthy in the North through their business interests, but the concept of getting rich is not in the lexicon of the co-operatives. Bill had many opportunities that might have made him rich, but he turned them down because he thought they were opportunities the community should take advantage of. He has a heart as big as all outdoors, and he is committed to helping people. The work that he has done for the co-operatives in the time that I have known him is monumental. He truly believes that his people have to be strong at the community level and that they don't have to rely on anybody else for what they want to do.

Another thing about Bill is that he says "yes" to every opportunity. He travels extensively wherever the federation needs him to go. Over the years he has had to deliver difficult messages to many different communities, when their co-operatives weren't doing well. One of the features of a co-operative is that it is an independent, community-owned and -controlled business. What the business is and how its members run it is up to them. Sometimes Bill has had to go to a community and tell them they need to take better charge of things. In those cases, he has to tell them that the federation cannot help them until they do something about their problems themselves.

The federation allows co-operatives to pool their buying power and their resources to help develop new facilities, but if a co-operative gets into trouble, because they aren't collecting their receivables, for example, they are putting other co-operatives at risk. When that happens, Bill goes in quickly to tell them that they are jeopardizing our entire co-op system. He also fields a lot of telephone calls from co-ops that are having problems with a director or a manager. He will help them find the resources they need to deal with the matter.

Sometimes Bill has to deliver tough replies to co-ops that are asking Arctic Co-operatives Ltd for money to develop. For example, sometimes a co-operative wants to build a new store but they are not doing well and don't have the money to build one. They think Arctic Co-operatives Ltd will give them a store, but that is not how the system works. You have to develop your own store, and Arctic Co-operatives Ltd will support you with resources and technical assistance. We have construction people and we have people who can help arrange financing, but if you can't raise your part of the money we can't help you borrow money. Bill has to tell them to get their business in order and save some money first; then we can stand with them before a financial institution or a governmental body. Bill encourages co-ops to base their thinking today on what they are going to do next year and in the coming years.

The Struggle to Survive

As the amalgamation of the federations was taking place in the early 1980s, we were in desperate financial shape, on the verge of bankruptcy. Our only priority was survival. At the time, from around 1983 to 1986, I was the financial controller of CACFL, and Andrew Goussaert was the chief executive officer. We had no money, we had no cash flow, and yet our job was to continue providing services. We had an unbelievably difficult time paying our bills. We would pay whoever we could on a given day and look for a way to pay somebody else the next day.

The Northwest Territories government of the time was very critical of the co-operatives. They offered a lot of advice but very little in the way of solutions. The government was particularly critical of Andrew Goussaert, who is actually a very calm, very thoughtful individual who was well liked across the North. My personal opinion is that the government didn't like that these co-operatives had a greater influence in communities than they did. We were being criticized constantly for everything, but we felt that if we responded to those unfounded statements, we would give credence to them. We tried to keep a low profile, because we just wanted to do our jobs, assist sister co-operatives, become stronger, and try to run successful businesses.

When the co-operatives decided to form a federation in 1972, they had no money. The members had a lot of heart and a lot of commitment, and they would each put up a couple of dollars to get things started, but there was no capital. One of the great drawbacks of the co-operative model is that it takes a long time to build capital. You have to be a business that can turn a profit in order to make that happen, but you can't start a profitable business if you don't have any capital. It is a catch-22 that meant the federation was always lacking money in the early years.

There were three major reasons why Arctic Co-operatives Ltd struggle to survive was so desperate: we were operating in a major economic recession that resulted in the devastation of the art industry; the fur industry was being destroyed by the international fur lobby; and interest rates were skyrocketing. The fact that our headquarters was located in Yellowknife didn't help us at all either.

There were a few major reasons why the NWT government didn't support us as much as they could have. The NWT government had supported the creation of the CACFL in 1972 with a small grant to get it started and to hire the first employees. The Eskimo Loan Fund of the Government of Canada provided $300,000, which was just not enough for us to provide our services. The financial plan that we had submitted to the Eskimo Loan Fund had called for a million dollars in capital, but with the influence of the NWT government, the federal government chose not to provide it. That meant they were undercapitalized co-operatives, in an undercapitalized federation, struggling to survive. By the end of the 1970s, we were operating in a major economic recession.

The recession of the late 1970s and 1980s that devastated the economy everywhere especially destroyed the art marketing industry. When people can't afford to put food on the table, they will not buy a carving. With that recession, interest rates skyrocketed. The prime rate in the early 1980s was in excess of twenty percent. Co-operatives had no capital, and because they had no equity they had difficulty borrowing. They relied heavily on supplier credit and small lines of credit from the banks. The interest rates on supplier credit and lines of credit are prime plus, so co-ops were paying twenty-two, twenty-three, twenty-four percent interest on their borrowings. They couldn't afford it, and they were being destroyed. They couldn't pay their bills.

On top of that, the international fur lobby was very effective in its opposition to the seal industry in Atlantic Canada. Ostensibly, they were not opposed to subsistence hunters, but their lobbying destroyed the fur industry for Inuit hunters who used to sell seal skins. Families from the Western Arctic who would work their trap lines for two or three months and come back at Christmas to sell their furs suddenly couldn't find buyers anymore. With fur and art as the only sources of income for most Inuit, the loss of those markets meant that there was no longer much money being circulated in the communities. Members couldn't afford to buy products from the local co-operatives. It was a tough time to do business.

Unfortunately, the board of directors of the CACFL had to make a few tough decisions. We had to tell the co-ops with low chances of survival that we couldn't support them anymore. Three or four co-operatives ended up closing their doors. It was heartbreaking. They didn't have the capital from the original Eskimo Loan Fund and we didn't have the money to support everybody. Everybody would have failed if the board hadn't made these tough decisions.

There was criticism of our federation from every side. The federal government wasn't as vocal as the NWT government, but people on the street would also criticize the very existence of the co-operatives. They didn't understand what we were doing. The board of directors had to take a hard look at how to fix the situation and make some tough decisions to try and get the network under control. If there were three things that devastated the Arctic co-operatives, there were also three that turned them around. The first was when the federation decided on a clear mandate to assist all these little co-operatives to develop business plans, implement the plans, and become more successful in running their businesses.

The second thing was that the federation began searching for another place to do business, a place where we could afford to operate. With our headquarters in Yellowknife, we really struggled to survive. We struggled to provide services because we couldn't keep staff.

We were competing for human resources with mining companies, such as Giant and Cominco, who could pay higher salaries than we could. We were also competing against the territorial government. The salaries of co-op employees were very low compared to everywhere else. We would hire accountants and buyers, but after a year they would leave us to go work for the territorial government for twenty-five percent more money. We went to the territorial government and told them that if we were to stay in Yellowknife we would need some support. They refused, and so our board of directors recommended that we find an alternative. Raising our prices wasn't an option, because that would put prices up at the community level. We began looking at relocating our offices.

It made sense to consider a southern location for our headquarters, because from there we would have better access to all points north. We went to a number of different provincial governments and asked them if they would support us if we moved to their province. They all declined. We started making plans to move to Ottawa, where our art marketing division, Canadian Arctic Producers, had its marketing showroom at the airport, in a 25,000-square-foot building. We had an annual general meeting and the members approved, and we notified our staff that we would be relocating our offices over a three-month period.

A short time later, we got a frantic call from the Manitoba government telling us they would like to reconsider about us relocating to Winnipeg. They flew in to Yellowknife that same night for a meeting! That night and the next morning we met with the minister of finance, the minister of co-operatives, and a department director. When they left Yellowknife by noon the next day, they were formulating an offer of a support package that would assist us in moving to Manitoba. Our board of directors reconsidered its decision and decided that we would relocate to Winnipeg rather than Ottawa. The Province of Manitoba would pay for our moving costs.

So, in 1985 we sold our building in Ottawa, we put our building in Yellowknife up for sale, and we moved all our staff from Ottawa and Yellowknife to Winnipeg. We moved our art marketing division to Winnipeg as well, where we maintained an art marketing showroom for another twelve years, until 1997. For a while, we had a showroom in Toronto, in partnership with the FCNQ from Northern Quebec, although we later agreed to disband that partnership. [6] In 1997 we moved our art marketing division to Toronto. [7]

For years after we relocated to Winnipeg, we were continually criticized by the NWT government for moving the co-operatives out of the territory. On top of that, our relationship with our financial institutions changed and became more difficult. All of these pressures made life hard for our delegates and directors. They were openly criticized for abandoning the North.

The move of our head office to Winnipeg was essentially the completion of our amalgamation. When we moved to Winnipeg in 1985, Arctic Co-operatives Limited truly came together. Fifteen years later, a delegate presented a resolution at our 2000 annual general meeting asking for an analysis of whether we had made the right decision to move. We hired somebody to examine our operations of the previous fifteen years and tell us what the impact of the move was. We learned that we were doing significantly better than we had ever done previously. The report concluded that by operating from Winnipeg instead of Yellowknife, the federation had saved $19 million in operating costs. We didn't even factor in the marketing! We calculated that the cost of that $19 million over a fifteen-year period was another $19 million, making a total savings of $38 million over a fifteen-year period.

6. FCNQ: Fédération des co-opératives du Nouveau-Québec. See http://www.fcnq.ca.
7. Canadian Arctic Producers is now located at 2891 Slough Street, Mississauga, Ontario.

When the board of directors received the final report, they decided the case was closed. The matter would not need to be discussed any more. We had made a good business decision and the benefits went right back to our member co-operatives in terms of patronage refund. We provided some parts of the report to the territorial government and told them we would not be talking about the issue again. The job of the federation is to provide the most efficient and effective services to our member co-operatives, and that is what we did.

The third thing that greatly improved our position was the creation of the Arctic Co-operative Development Fund, our financial arm. In 1984, the government of Canada came up with a program called the Native Economic Development Program (NEDP). It was created because the federal government recognized that a lack of capital was a serious problem for aboriginal businesses across Canada. They wanted to create pools of capital for average businesses to grow and develop. Our co-operatives decided that our model was an ideal one for the program.

That model had been tested in the 1970s, when the federation would make applications to the Eskimo Loan Fund on behalf of various co-operatives. In the early 1970s we had approached the Eskimo Loan Fund, which was ready to make loans and grants to individual co-operatives, and asked them to make the loans to the federation instead. In turn, we would then lend to our member co-ops that applied to us for funding. That way, these co-ops could repay the federation in reasonable instalments, with no interest. Once the loan was paid back, the federation would lend that money to somebody else. That mechanism was known as the Co-operative Development Fund. Over time, money built up in this fund, and by the early 1980s we had $50,000 in capital in the Eskimo Loan Fund. The Co-operative Development Fund started with a little bit of money, small loans, and slow payments, and the money came back. It did an awful lot of good for the local co-ops.

In 1984, when the Native Economic Development Program (NEDP) started, that collective model was the one we used to submit an application for funding. We went through all the co-operatives' operations, determined what kind of capital was needed, and submitted an application based on these numbers. Our total request was for $30 million. The NEDP people took our application under review and hired consultants to analyze our co-ops and our Arctic Co-operatives Ltd operations. The process dragged on, probably because the NWT government didn't like that NEDP was interested in our application. The Department of Indian and Northern Affairs was involved, but the NWT government was decidedly not.

We were back in the bad books of the territorial government because in 1982, the NWT government still owned a factory in Inuvik that was called Inuvik Parka Enterprises. The government wanted to privatize it and encouraged Arctic Co-operatives Ltd to buy it. We were interested because we thought it would make a wonderful worker co-operative, with Inuvik women working in the factory and selling their parkas. We evaluated the financial statements and felt that the business had a certain kind of value, so we agreed to purchase Inuvik Parka Enterprises. After we agreed to buy it we got a revised financial statement that was different from the one the purchase was based on. We went back to the territorial government, and they were not happy to see us. That added a little more fuel to our difficult relationship with them. On top of that, one of our major customers, the HBC, suddenly stopped buying parkas from the company, so the business struggled from day one. By 1985, when the NEDP was launching, we were trying to resolve this whole issue with the Inuvik Parka Enterprises.

The NEDP was a program of Industry Canada. The Department of Northern and Indian Affairs was also quite heavily involved, and they were all ready to consider that Arctic Co-operatives Ltd might be a good recipient of the NEDP funds. They had already provided us with a loan guarantee, and that guarantee helped to finance inventory. They were pressuring the NWT government to get involved with some money, but our relationship with them was difficult: we had left Yellowknife, and we were having these challenging discussions about Inuvik Parka Enterprises. Ultimately, on April 7, 1986, the Arctic Co-operative Development Fund was incorporated. It was launched with $10.2 million of capital and the agreement of the NWT government that they would buy back Inuvik Parka Enterprises. They chose not to work with us to fix it, so they bought it back and gave it away.

The NWT government and the Department of Indian Affairs did not believe that Arctic Co-operatives Ltd could manage this. They felt that the Arctic Co-op Development Fund had to be a separate entity, located in Yellowknife. The NEDP put in $5 million in new cash, and the Eskimo Loan Fund at Indian Affairs transferred to us the loans of $4.9 million that were associated with the line of credit that they had guaranteed, and the NWT government put in $300,000 in cash. That was a major step forward because the co-operatives now had a source of capital. Prior to that we couldn't even afford to pay for our re-supply inventory. Re-supply is the once-a-year supply of products that goes in by ship and that doesn't get sold for 12 to 16 months.

That first year, we financed $2 million worth of inventory. This year, we will be at about $28 million worth of inventory on re-supply. Now, we can have product leave our suppliers for the docks so it can be shipped in early summer. From the co-ops in the communities, it will be sold over the following twelve months. That means we have a lead time of fifteen months for products and for financing, whereas before we didn't have the capital to do that. Now, we can lend several million dollars for inventory. We can actually approve orders and have the money to pay for them.

A young team

Back when Bill was the president of the board of directors and Andrew Goussaert was the chief executive officer, I was the financial controller of Arctic Co-operatives Ltd. I was just in my early thirties, with limited experience. We worked together well, though. Andrew was a visionary, and Bill was a motivator. Bill can gather people together and get them going. I really believe in what he does.

Sometimes, in those early days, I had no idea where to turn to find the money needed to stay in business until the next day. I would go into Andrew's office and we would talk for two or three hours and I would leave the office all fired up. A day or two later I would think, "He did it to me again: nothing's changed. He just got me motivated and got me going!" There were no obvious solutions, but he motivated us to think about the little things that made it worthwhile.

We had many bad days. At least we were young and naïve enough not to know how serious the problem was. We were struggling to stay in business ourselves, yet we had all these other co-ops depending on us, their federation. If we went out of business, most of the member co-ops would go too, because they had no capital. We wheeled and dealt with our suppliers, giving them a little bit of money so they would ship inventory, and we did acrobatics to try and make one more payroll.

To have a visionary like Andrew with us was pivotal to our present success, and we needed Bill out there building support. Politically, Bill was very well known at that point. He had been an MLA, he had been on the board of the Eskimo Loan Fund, and he had been on the NWT Water Board. He had also been invited by the federal government to serve on the board of directors of the Native Economic Development Program right from the beginning. The fact that Bill was in these circles and was able to talk about co-operatives made these people understand what we were and what we were doing. He was also involved in the national co-operative movement, at a time when we were trying to gain acceptance from other co-operatives in the country. Bill and Andrew would represent us at the annual meetings of Federated Co-operatives Limited and the Co-operative Union of Canada, now the Canadian Co-operative Association. We also used to send people from the Arctic to the Co-op College in Saskatoon.[8] There are many prominent people in the North who attended programs there.

With the big financial improvements we could make in our business with the Co-operative Development Fund, we could now worry about developing co-operatives, not just surviving. It allowed us to experience a big change in our thinking, too. For a number of years we had tried to stay out of the media, because we couldn't afford any negative press. If some entity criticized us, we chose not to respond and prolong the affair. Then, ten years ago, we decided that while that had helped us get through a difficult period in our history, now we would have to come out of the shadows and start promoting ourselves. Today, we have a wonderful story to tell.

We were years ahead of our time in some of the co-op training and education that took place. We used to produce cassette tapes about co-operatives in multiple languages and provide them to local community radio stations. In the 1970s and '80s, we were doing our own version of distance education through teleconferencing: every one of our member co-operatives had a little microphone, like those for radio announcers, with a speaker attached, and with them we could teleconference with four or five people

---

8. The Co-operative College of Canada had its roots in the 1940s and 1950s Western co-op movement. The institute offered management and other co-operative-based training until it closed its doors in 1987. Upon closing, it merged with the Co-operative Union of Canada to form the Canadian Co-operative Association. See: http://esask.uregina. ca/entry/co-operative_college_of_canada.html.

around the table, plus people from four or five remote sites. We offered them management and board of directors training. We still have a training department today, but it used to be much larger, with trainers developing material specific to our needs.

We were years ahead of our time, years ahead of our financial capacity, and years ahead from a visionary standpoint because training was such a critical part of our growth. Training is also a critical part of our future. The big thing we have to be working on is training and development and education. The co-ops were the first development corporations—in the earliest days, there was nothing before and beside the co-ops. They helped to build the communities.

One of the most inspiring early co-op stories is about how Pelly Bay built their runway. They had received some community development money from the territorial government and decided that they wanted to build a runway. It was the only community at the time that couldn't be re-supplied by ship. To build the runway, they used some equipment that they had salvaged from a DEW Line site about fifty miles away. Everybody in the community worked on the project, and they used some of the development money to pay them. They chose to pay people based on what they needed. If someone had a wife and four children and another person had a wife and one child, the man with a bigger family received more money. They spread the money out.

They built a runway that was able to handle C-130 aircraft, and then the Koomiut Co-op bought a DC-4 aircraft. Willie Lazarus was a partner and the chief pilot. At the time, the NWT government was supporting the development of commercial airlines with regularly scheduled routes, so they were against the purchase of the co-op's DC-4. Obviously, all the other co-ops wanted to use the plane to have supplies brought in, but because the Koomiut Co-op didn't have a commercial license, legally,

they weren't allowed to service them. The co-op got around
that problem by purchasing the supplies in their own name,
flying them into the community, and selling the goods to
the local co-op once on the ground. Technically, they were
not transporting anybody else's goods!

All this played a role in the 1972 discussions about
forming a federation. All the co-ops talked for days about
the pros and the cons. Although they recognized the
need for better services, they didn't want to give up their
autonomy and independence. Finally, the Koomiut Co-op
proposed to sell their airplane to the federation. That move
swayed the discussion, because access to the plane would
be an undeniable benefit of being part of the federation.

The development of the co-operative movement in the
North happened because the right people were there at the
right time. Andrew mentored Bill Lyall and encouraged
him to become involved in the co-op movement. The more
involved Bill became, the more enamoured he was with the
whole concept and the more his leadership skills came into
play. If you look at the federation today, compared to when
Bill first became involved, there is no comparison. Bill has
been the elected leader nearly that whole time. He has been
President of Arctic Co-operatives Limited almost straight
through since 1981 and President of the Co-operative
Development Fund since it was incorporated. If we are in
a strong position today, it is, in large part, because Bill has
been solidly advocating for us the whole time.

Arctic Co-operative Movement Timeline

1959   The first community based Co-operatives were incorporated.

1965   Canadian Arctic Producers (CAP) was incorporated as a limited company by 12 producer Co-operatives and the Government of Canada to market the arts and crafts of local Co-ops.

1972   The Canadian Arctic Co-operative Federation Limited (CACFL) was incorporated by 26 community based Co-operatives in February 1972 to provide support services to local Co-ops.

1979   Canadian Arctic Producers was restructured as a Co-operative, Canadien Arctic Producers Co-operative Limited (CAPCL)

1981   Arctic Co-operatives Limited (Arctic Co-operatives Ltd) was incorporated to manage the amalgamation of CACFL/CAPCL.

1982   The formal amalgamation of CACFL/CAPCL/ Arctic Co-operatives Ltd was completed and Arctic Co-operatives Limited became the sole service federation of the Co-operatives of the Arctic.

1985   The service offices of Arctic Co-operatives Limited were relocated from Yellowknife and Ottawa to Winnipeg, MB.

1986   NWT Cooperative Business Development Fund (CBDF) was incorporated in April 1986 as the financial arm of the community based Co-operatives in the Arctic.

1999   CBDF was renamed as the Arctic Co-operative Development Fund (ACDF).

2003   The bylaws of Arctic Co-operative Development Fund were amended to provide that the Board of Directors of Arctic Co-operatives Limited would also serve as the Board of Director of ACDF.

2004   The service office of Arctic Co-operative Development Fund was consolidated in the Winnipeg service office of Arctic Co-operatives Limited.

References

Iglauer, Edith. 2000. Inuit Journey: The Co-operative Adventure in Canada's North, Madeira Park, British Columbia. North Harbour Publishing. 254 pages.

La Fédération des coopératives du Nouveau-Québec. 2007. Partager autrement, La petite histoire du mouvement cooperatif au Nunavik. Montréal. La Fédération des coopératives du Nouveau-Québec. 287 pages.

Lyall, Ernie. 1979. An Arctic Man. Edmonton. Hurtig Publishers. Published in paperback in 1983 by Goodread Biographies. 239 pages.

Mitchell, Marybelle. 1996. From Talking Chiefs to a Native Corporate Elite, The Birth of Class and Nationalism among Canadian Inuit. Montreal-Kingston. McGill-Queen's University Press. 533 pages.

Mowat, Farley. 1984. The Snow Walker. Seal Books; Reissue edition (Nov. 1 1984) Stackpole Books. Mechanicsburg. 224 pages.

Partridge, Shannon (Editor). 2009. Niurrutiqarniq, Trading with the Hudson's Bay Company. Iqaluit. Nunavut Arctic College. 279 pages.

Statistics Canada. 2010. An analysis of the housing needs in Nunavut: Nunavut Housing Needs Survey 2009/2010. Nunavut Housing Corporation. http://www.stats.gov.nu.ca/Publications/Housing/NHNS%20Pubs/Analysis%20of%20the%20Housing%20Needs%20in%20Nunavut,%202009-2010.pdf

Index